B.A.R.E.

Being Alone Reveals Emotion

Written By: L. D. Lovejoy

*A compilation of spoken word poems
Written and performed by
L. D. Lovejoy*

To whomever this makes feel whole again, love again, and find one's way ...

B.A. R. E.
Being alone reveals emotion

L.D.Lovejoy

Preface : A letter to my loves

We've all been here before , that feeling of feeling unappreciated, used, abused , mislead and confused ... sometimes we don't even know how to put most situations into words , we bottle up our emotions and some of us even go into solitude, I chose to write it out , it always made me feel like if nobody heard me speaking than at least these white pages and fainted lines will know my truths.

I stripped myself naked , I no longer wanted to lie to myself to please others , I questioned my reasons , my faults and my emotions .I cried plenty of nights , cause being alone really reveals emotion and if you've been there before this one's for you.

I give my love because I too was once where you are sitting right now, because I too made decisions based off my vulnerable ways, because I too did to please others but forgot that loving myself was more powerful than draining myself. I have always been afraid to let my light shine because I was always busy dimming my light to share with others. So, what happens when that bitter taste starts to taste sweet, let's talk about it . . .

I always was the advice giver, the love seeker, the one who would tell others to live, love and try again. I always wanted to be the peacemaker and always had that ear to listen. I never really had many ask me "are you okay" or "how are you", most times I had to deal with my emotions on my own, I always journaled, I always jotted down exactly how someone made me feel when I showed I didn't care, but did.

I had bad habits I couldn't break, I picked up on bad habits from others and lost myself and my innocence along the way, I didn't know who I really was anymore or who I wanted to be, and my emotions were connected to soul ties, that were connected to more soul ties that were no longer connected to me. I was not showed how to love properly, nor did I let that write my story. I taught myself to love by asking myself "if you want to be loved like this, how can you exude love, how can you give love and how can you be love"

I can admit I wasn't always the best lover, because I never had the opportunity to feel and let my feelings be felt, I will let my mind race with thoughts and act out on those without compromise without understanding without reason. I encouraged myself to heal from the inside out, but I never really knew what I was healing from, I would ask myself was it something I was missing from my childhood or was it something instilled inside of me. I do not have all the answers, but I have these emotions to share with many who may have put up the same fight.

So here I let go of my fears and tears, I want to say thank you. To you. for allowing me to be transparent and open, for encouraging me to step out of my own self and reaching outside of my box, I am grateful that you believed in me enough to hear my truths that I saw as weaknesses,
So this is for you.

I give my Love,
L.D. Lovejoy

A genuine love that pours into others effortlessly, A soul that is not searching for nothing but to be the gift, the taste many will search for but will not get their hands on, the seasoning, the chosen one, the recipe

~ Soul Food

SPEAK:

It's not the fact that I don't cook, or curl my own hair

There's no ring on my finger , but you expect me to take it there ..
You want me to listen to your wants , minor changes and needs
But when I ask you to straighten up , you do as you please ...

Are we committed here?, or are you enjoying your time? , is this temporary love? , cause I don't have that type of time

I love out loud , patiently and secure , so a hidden love is a forbidden love , speak up now, if your love is unsure .

Listen to me for once , I won't ask that again ; a hidden love is a forbidden love , I'll damn sure repeat that again.

So it's not the fact I don't cook or curl my own hair , if you don't see me in your future can you tell me "why are you here?"

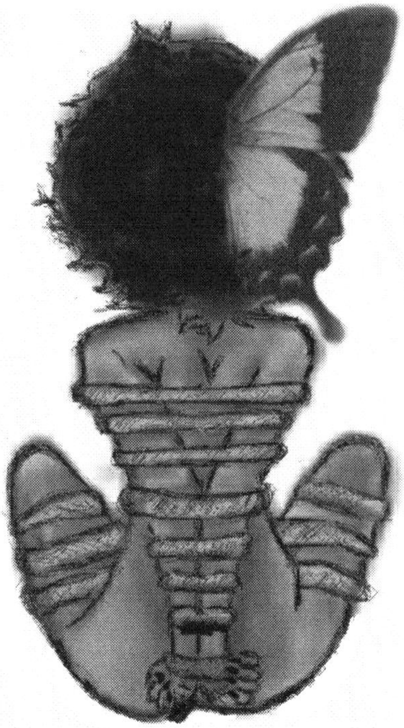

~ The best advice is the advice of your own. Trust it. You can be too attached to something that has already served its purpose in your life, trust your gut and dead everything that is not serving you.

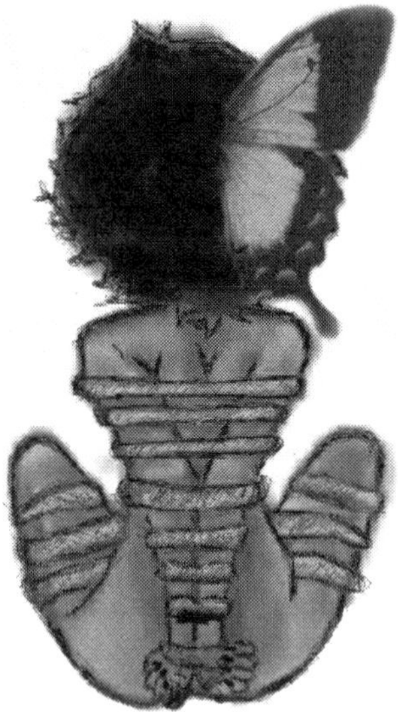

Closed Coffins:

Today I wrote dummy on my forehead , outlined with lip liner and drawn with ruby woo , once I start explaining, you'll get it from my point of view :

they will take advantage of you , they said
They will only benefit from you, They said

And even though I heard those words time and time again ,
I didn't want to read between the lines .....
cause my help so genuine, I make anybody's problems mine

What's it like to be used ? Not once ... not a few times,

but when you feel like everyone you meet, heard about your helping hand through the grapevines

Do you want to be my lover or do you want to be my friend, there's not a human soul I can trust, without thinking "Am I being used again."

I can't get close to people, so my friends are few... and every guy I meet, they tend to leave after a few pair of shoes.

So now you see my reason, it wouldn't hurt me if you agreed, I tend to pour into many cups that never pour into me ...

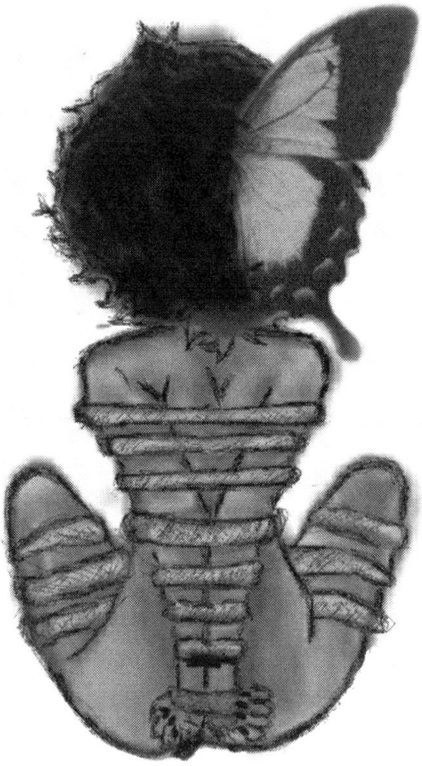

Clift Hanger:

I never intended to hurt you, but your intent was to go into over kill
I was blinded by the lies which corrupted how I felt.

You played a dangerous game, when all I wanted was to play fair, damn who hurt you, they really left no hope there,

I wanted to heal you, I made your problems mine from the start, I whispered sweet melodies in your ear, I uplifted you when it came to doing my part, I protected you when my friends said you were no good..

Well Mr. know it all let's get something understood, I won't cry because you didn't see my worth, I won't dwell cause you missed out on me sir ..

and first of all Mr. know it all, I've laid in these sheets before, I hope your next girl be better than your last girl .. cause my intentions were never to hurt you, but it seems you have used a few women before.

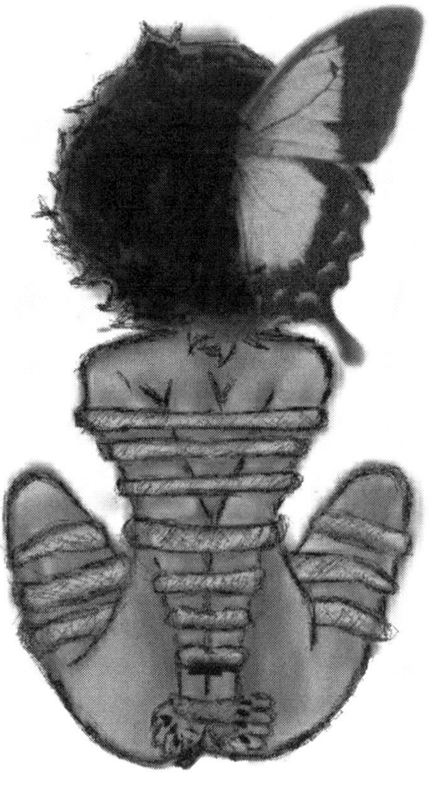

I could write a memoir on how people use the tool of distraction to run away from their problems and fears

Suppressing your emotions does not mean you are healed. It means you are neglecting your feelings and causing further damage.

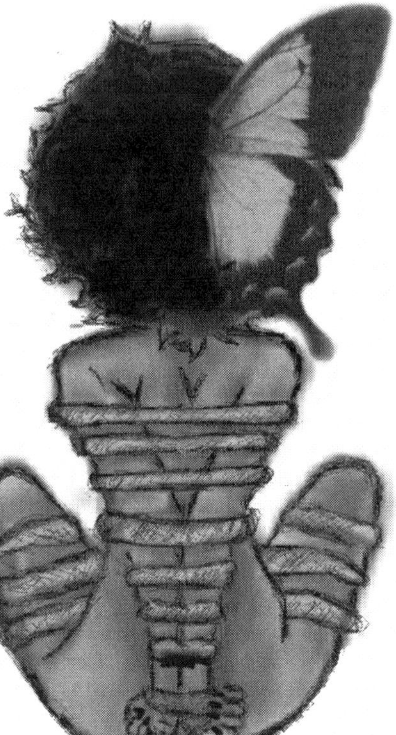

10 things I'll tell my therapists:

1. You think I am stuck inside of my own head; you think I am surrounded by my own insecurities, but I will be damned to put that blame on me.
2. I did not choose to be empathetic this life chose me, a big heart, many scars but I still find love in the smallest things.
3. Why is my silence so loud but you will never hear me weep, they box me in as the strong one, the independent one like I don't grow weak.
4. I get tired sometimes too, I cannot always find the right words to say, the wrong things can make someone feel like I am condescending, demeaning, demanding, wait please stay.
5. I did not mean to get aggressive I am passive yet sure, I am speaking from a dark place, have you been here before?
6. I did it again, yes, it is like me to take control, venting here felt safe when I am no longer playing a role.
7. Strip me naked, let me be free. I have always felt uncomfortable opening to anybody that was not me.
8. The purest form of love is one that you can accept on your own, with no conditions, no limits with a genuine soul.
9. I put my guard up cause my trust is far and few. If I am surrounded by my own insecurities how did I open to you.
10. I let myself down because there is still so much more to say, but I allowed myself only 10 reasons I came to you today.

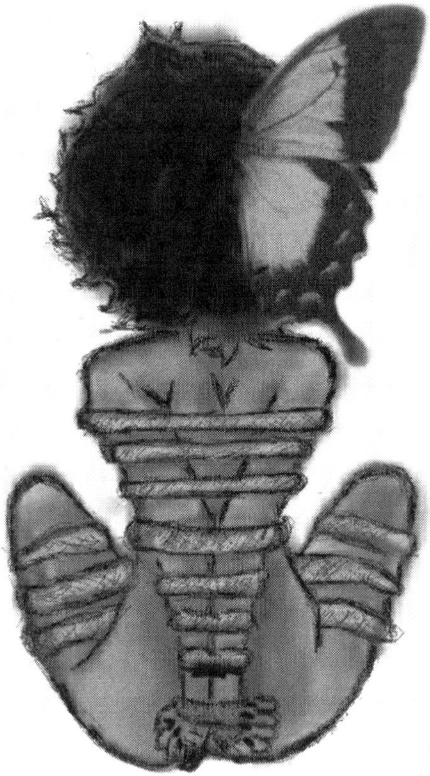

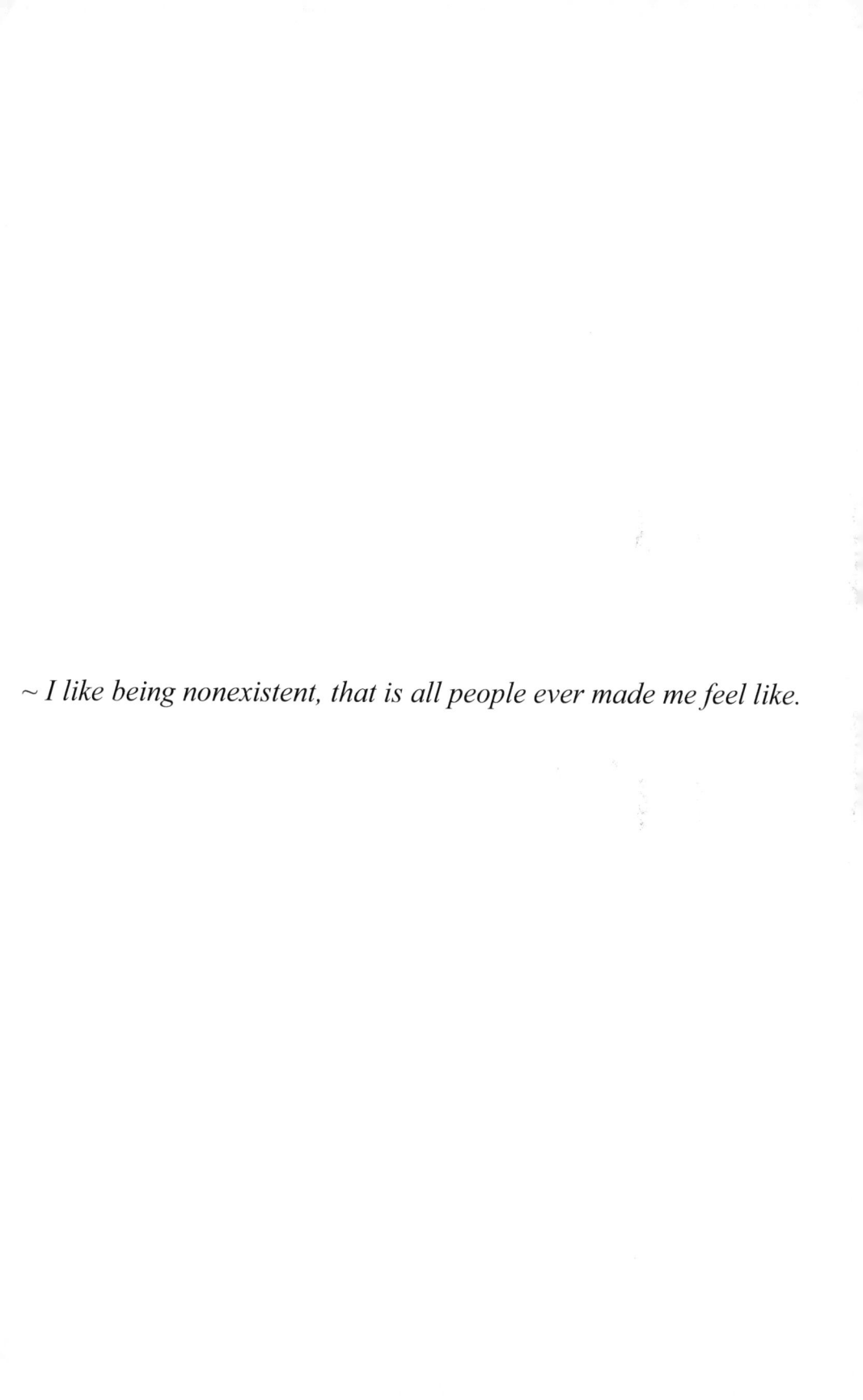

~ *I like being nonexistent, that is all people ever made me feel like.*

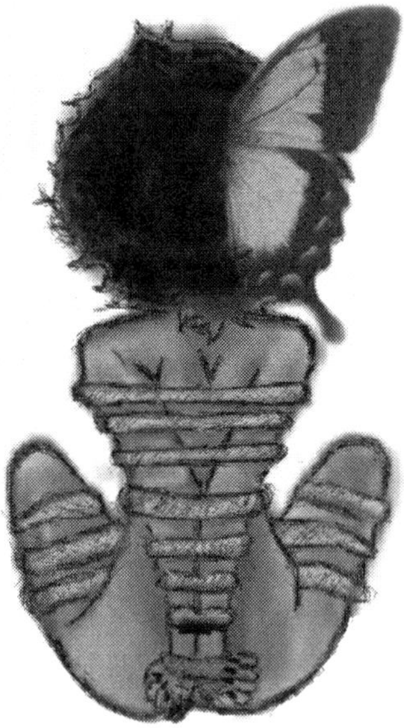

Questions:

*We crave an understanding of love, we rather have it mapped out, drawn out and given to us, but would you be okay with loving yourself, and never finding that soul mate, would you be okay with having so much love to give and never being able to give it ...
would you be ok?*

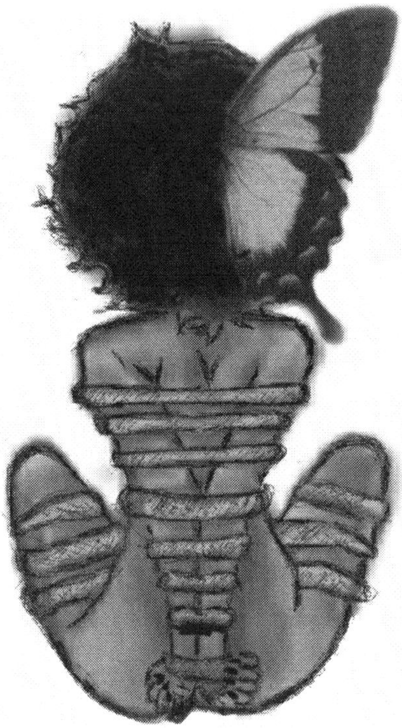

Footnotes:

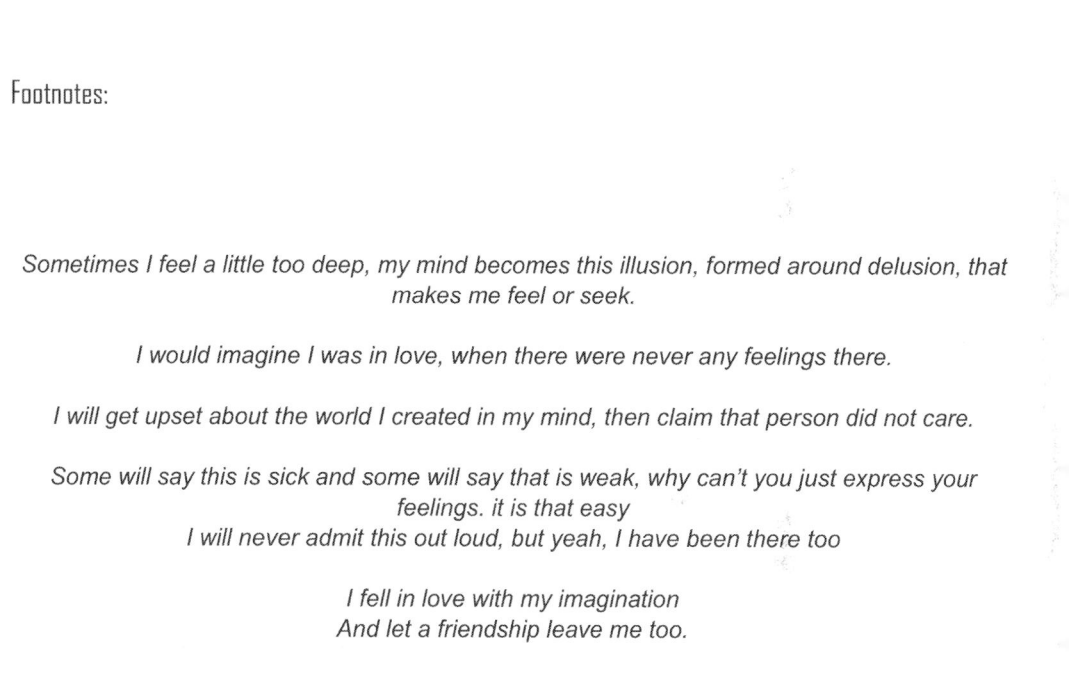

Sometimes I feel a little too deep, my mind becomes this illusion, formed around delusion, that makes me feel or seek.

I would imagine I was in love, when there were never any feelings there.

I will get upset about the world I created in my mind, then claim that person did not care.

Some will say this is sick and some will say that is weak, why can't you just express your feelings. it is that easy
I will never admit this out loud, but yeah, I have been there too

I fell in love with my imagination
And let a friendship leave me too.

But I deserved love.

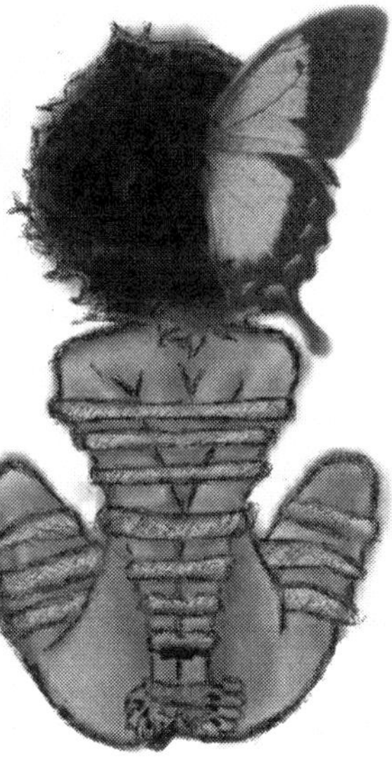

Her Story:

I don't want to be cliche with the why her and not me line , cause I wouldn't care if you wrote it out for me a million times, sworn yourself into secrecy or even just outed the words for me, your lies age like wine and it repeated itself like history

Does she know I got the privileges she only dreamed of , does she know I got to see you on the days she only would think of and somehow that makes me upset ..

I never wanted to be the other woman but I was here first and I just knew I was up next but .... in the back of your mind that is something that would never be. she was more deserving of a title while I was someone you told that "with you is where I rather be"

They say you have to love yourself enough to walk away, but somehow I convinced myself I loved myself enough to stay;
just let me explain :

If I gave up on us I knew for sure I would slip away, we put our trust in each other long enough to run the race, your smile started to be the reason mine still showed , your laugh started to be the reason mine was so bold , I couldn't walk away from a feeling like this, I'd lose myself completely and I knew it would end up just like this, I wasn't ready to break our bond, I wasn't ready to stop complaining about only seeing you 2 times a month , I wasn't ready ...

Today I pulled out my journal and the thought breathed you. I wrote out my emotions and the pages bled truths , I love myself enough to walk away because why would You want to be with someone who doesn't respect a love they have in the first place , why would you want to be with someone who had you but went searching for more , then made you the secret and gave her the front door , why would you want to be with someone who would never chose you , why would you want to be someone's little secret for nothing but a love no one ever knew?
You got to love yourself enough to know your worth is far more than lies, sex , and small visits from time to time .. you got to love yourself to know you do not want a love built off lies ...

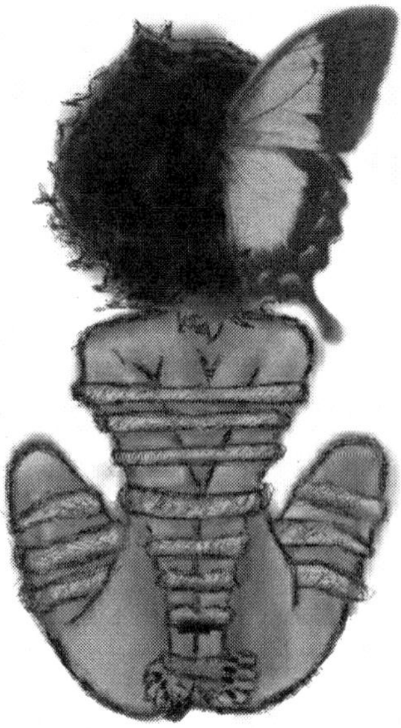

~ We as women must remember without men, we are enough.

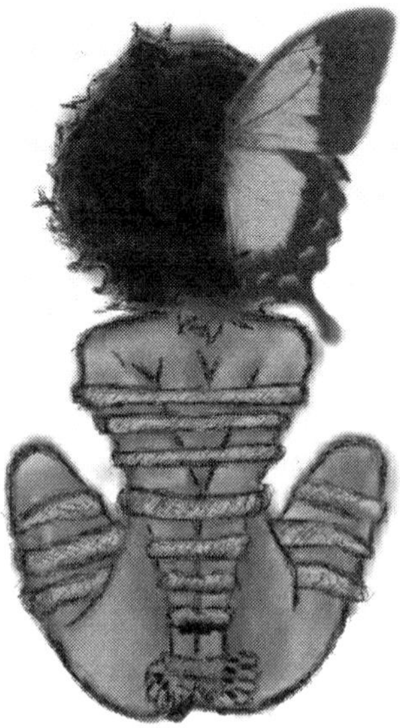

I have not had a night like this in so long, one that gets my blood rushing, my feet a tingling, my hands tip tapping, like I am perfecting a love song.

A night where my thoughts are free falling and open to be shared freely. a night where my feelings become weakened by a soul that crossed me, shook me, misplaced me enough to awake me, to speak like the book of psalms. I have not had a night like this in so long ...

You may have wondered where I been hiding out, and when everything got quiet, still wondered what the fuss was about. I have not had a night like this in so long.

you do not need validation. you owe yourself at-least this one thing. Feeling lonely In everybody else's world will have you creating your own. It almost felt impossible to me. I have not had a night like this in so long.

Reflect me.

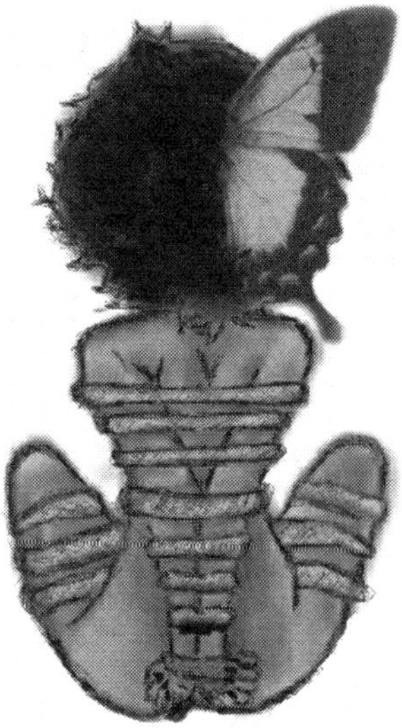

~ Most nights I reflect and wish I could have done more throughout the day to love harder from a distance.
Wish I did more to protect my personal space and emotions.

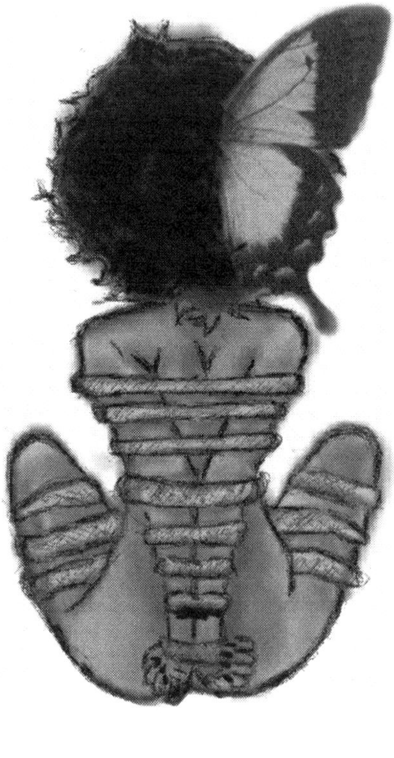

Slave:

It's been 30 days , seven hundred -twenty hours and some odd minutes and I'm still depicting apart the reasons you couldn't stay
It's the compare and contrast for me , it's the unreturned calls for me , it's the small lies that I made up in my mind cause I wanted us to be .

Why wasn't I enough for you,

why couldn't you just give me the closure cause that made my heart hold on a little longer I promise I wouldn't have lingered if you gave me the reasons you walked out and cheated , but then again ...

I never needed you less , I never wanted you less , I still look out the window hoping you'll come running back , cause I feel like I was the woman that changed your bad habits and maybe the pressure was too much for you so you wanted to test my love ,and damn I'll give you that but then again...

You couldn't see what you meant to me , I put you on a pedestal although you felt undeserving ..

I still uttered and cried in my sleep because somehow you still appear in my dreams , and maybe that closure was all I needed to understand men will do what they want to , and when they show you what they rather do don't ever feel less than , it's never your fault that a man couldn't be a man

But my body became a hostage to you.

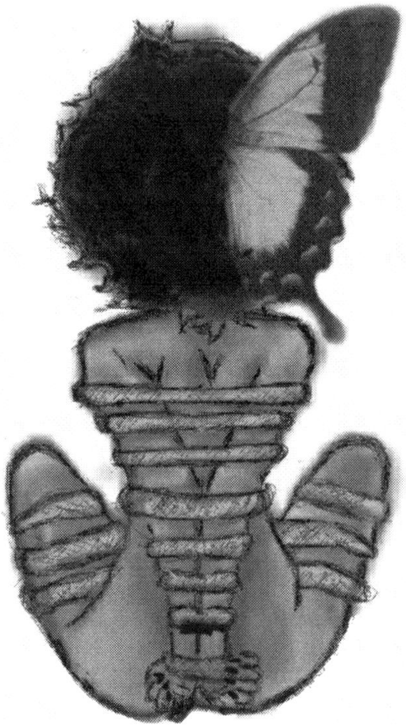

~ *The day I accept the fact, my love is far too deep for anyone to reciprocate is the day my problems will go away ....*

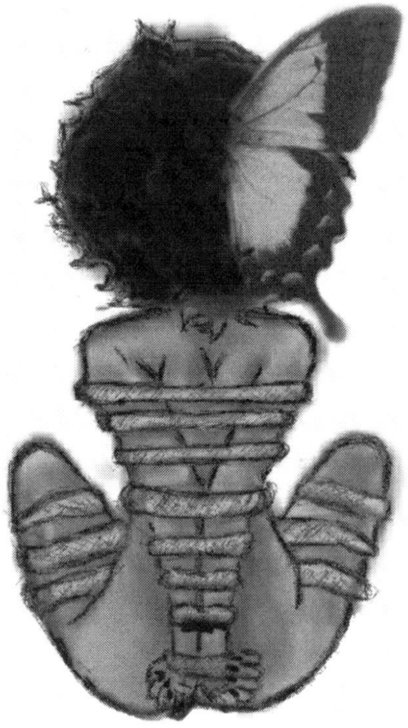

Message,

You must be careful when people know you are a giver, they fall in love with your hand instead of your heart EVERYTIME.

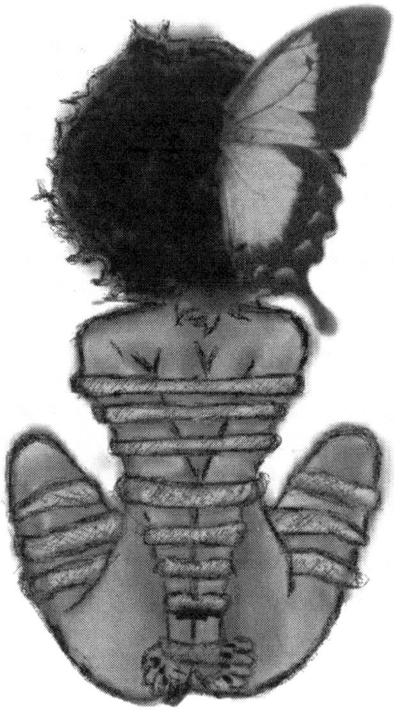

City view:

I have a bad habit of seeing the potential in someone who could've been .

You could've been great but let's not pretend -

I had to stretch out my neck to get a better view,

I had to understand people were more interested in "what's in it for you"

There had to be a handout or white lies told along the way , cause if they showed the real them too soon they knew I wouldn't stay ..

If they breathed in my love too deep they knew I would stray ,

I had to have just enough balance to feel in control

And sometimes I reserved just enough power to play the role

I was losing me .

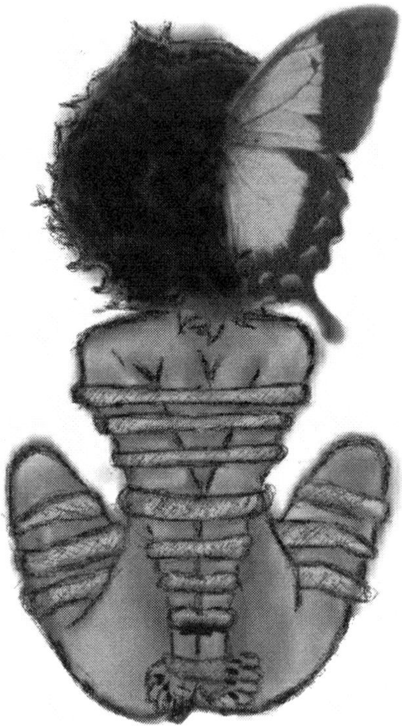

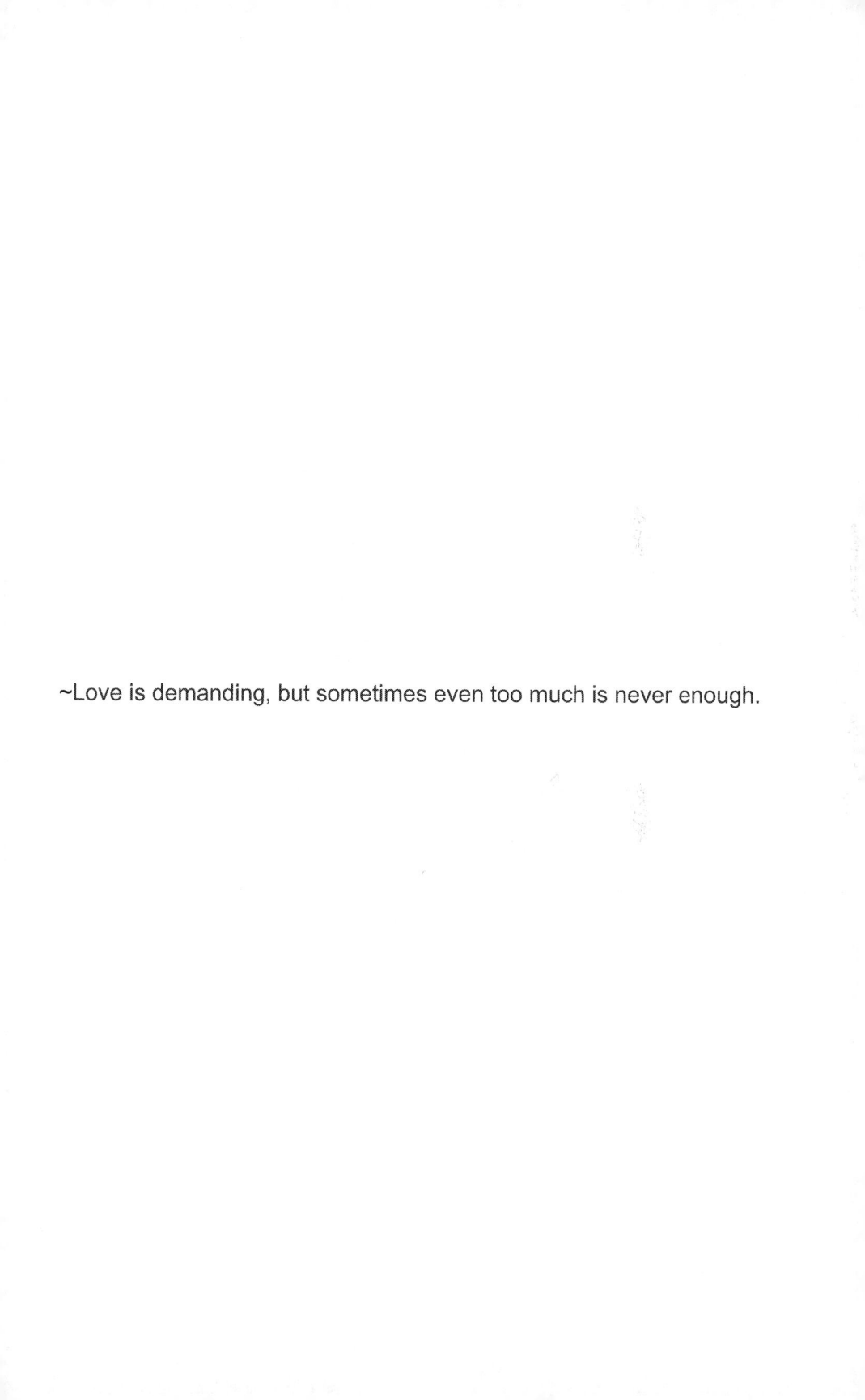

~Love is demanding, but sometimes even too much is never enough.

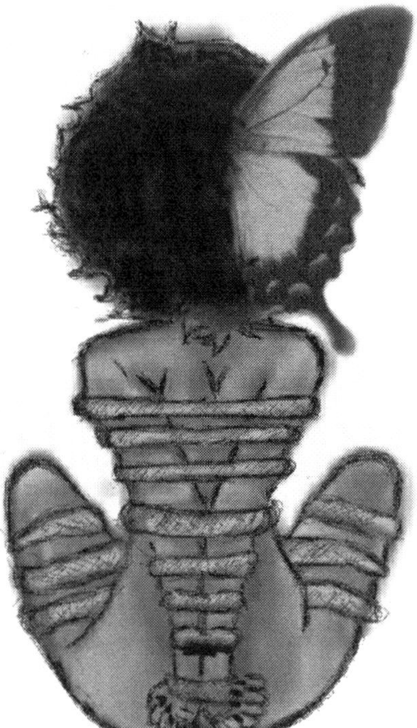

4:15am

I have been up for 13 days, scrolling through the albums in my camera roll, our playlist on repeat what happened to forever and forehead kisses, your nudes still bring back memories why chose now to leave?

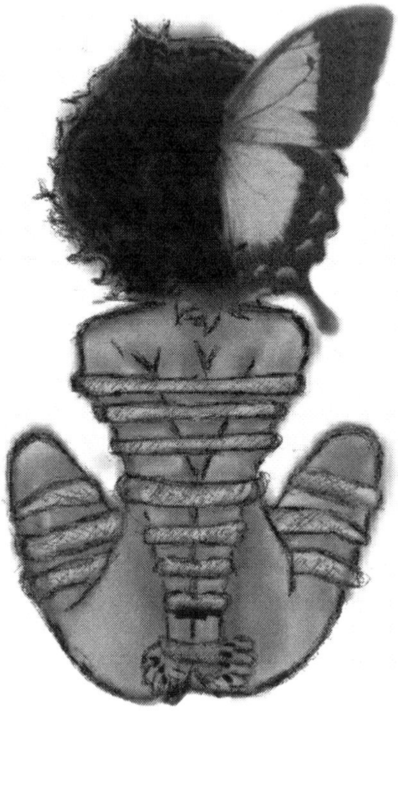

Losing Control:

To be so empathetic has to come with a reward , the emotions you have built up seems like it only builds to destroy

Who am I now in the present .
I no longer want to be stuck in my past , I no longer want to weep for a seat on the other side of a greener grass

I keep my problems to myself cause I'm no woe is me , but to be an emotional human , That's no facade to me

One that comes black and white with no in-betweens , one that if you speak too fast you might miss the loneliness that comes with me.

I've been drained for my love and still continued to love the same , I would say I don't care till I'm blue in the face but nobody could see my heart was sinking to my knees , nobody could see I was screaming for help through clenched teeth

Nobody wanted to hear my problems they just seen that it was give and take and every time it happened I no longer loved myself the same.

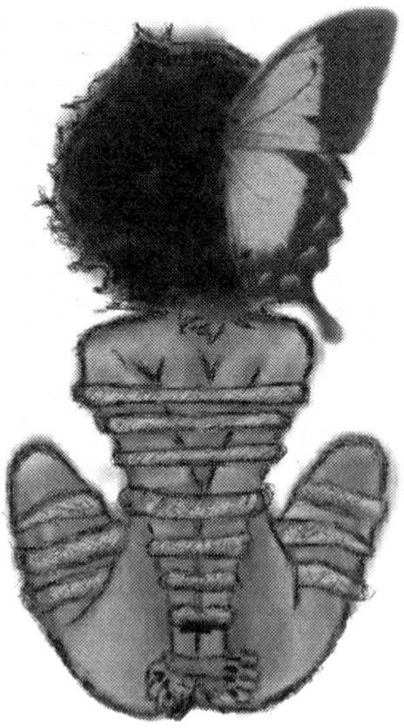

~ My soul will always be worth more than this world can offer.

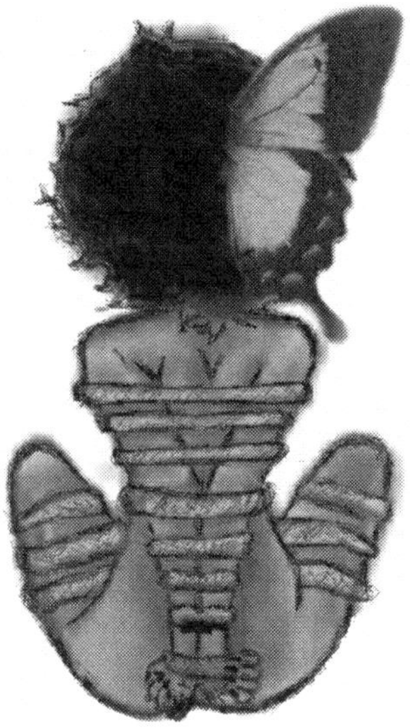

I had plans for us, remember how we came up with a baby name in 15 minutes? Hunter Elyse with your last name attached with it, we would talk for hours about living out loud, and how we will never leave each other, that shit seems so funny now.

I do not want to ever love again like this, cause if it makes me question myself even a little... was it ever really meant to give me a feel-good feeling or were we filling a void for just a minute ...

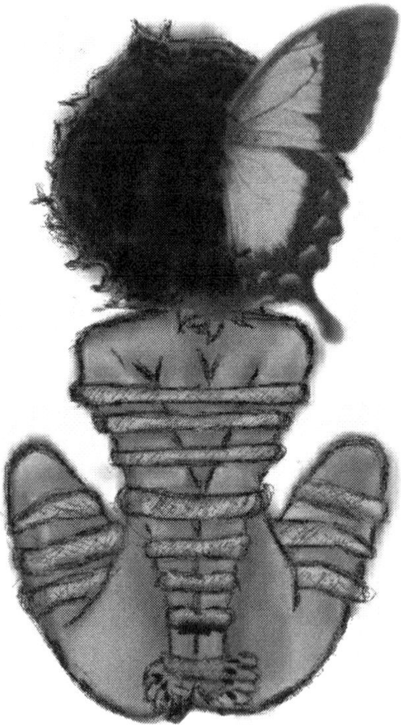

Small to You:

I tend to go where they always leave , and sometimes I feel like I'm alone , but I got me .

My solitude has never been so questionary but is it necessary to sit still with my emotions or drive down dark roads with verses and make up lullabies and sweet melodies .

Where did this all come from in the first place?

I never wanted to feel .

, I wanted to be numb waiting for our last days , and if nobody was proud of me I was proud of me cause no one really knew I was forced to live in my truth and no matter how dark my days would get it was me who had to fight to feel relevant in a world that made me feel smaller than James and that giant peach .

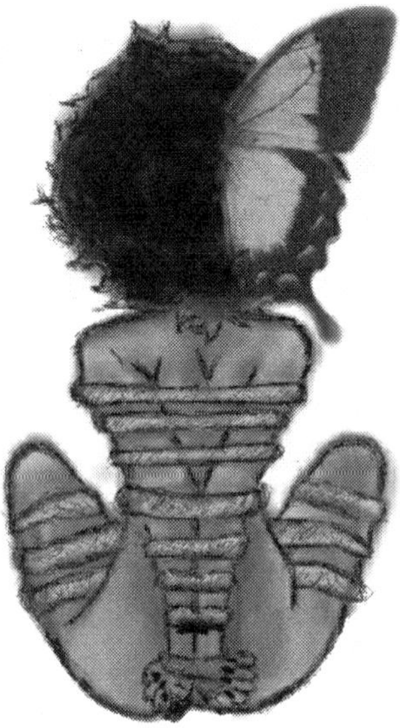

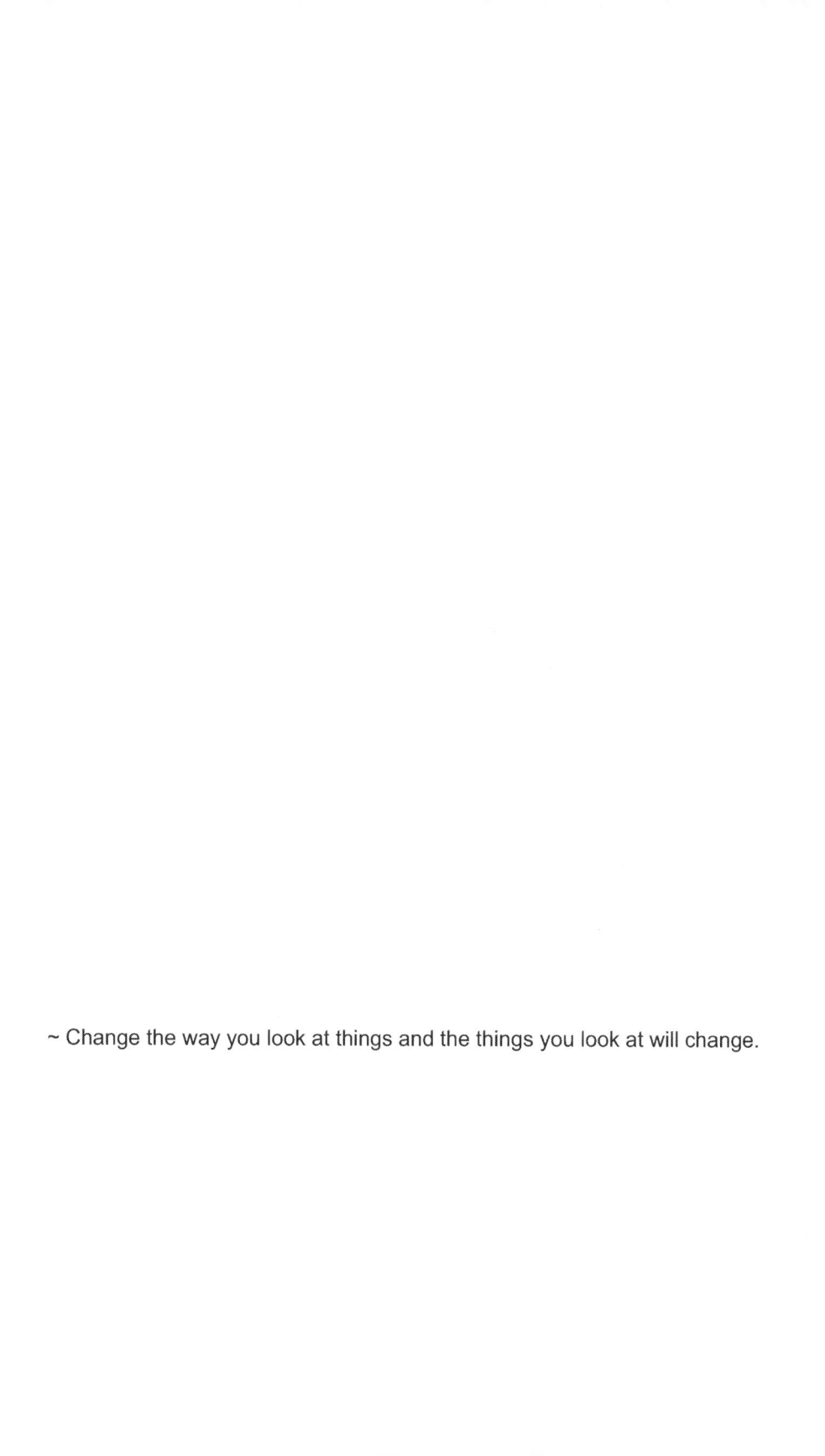

~ Change the way you look at things and the things you look at will change.

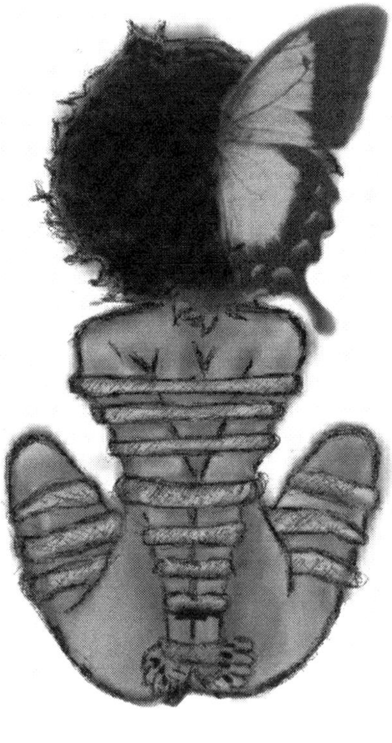

The Devil in Disguise:

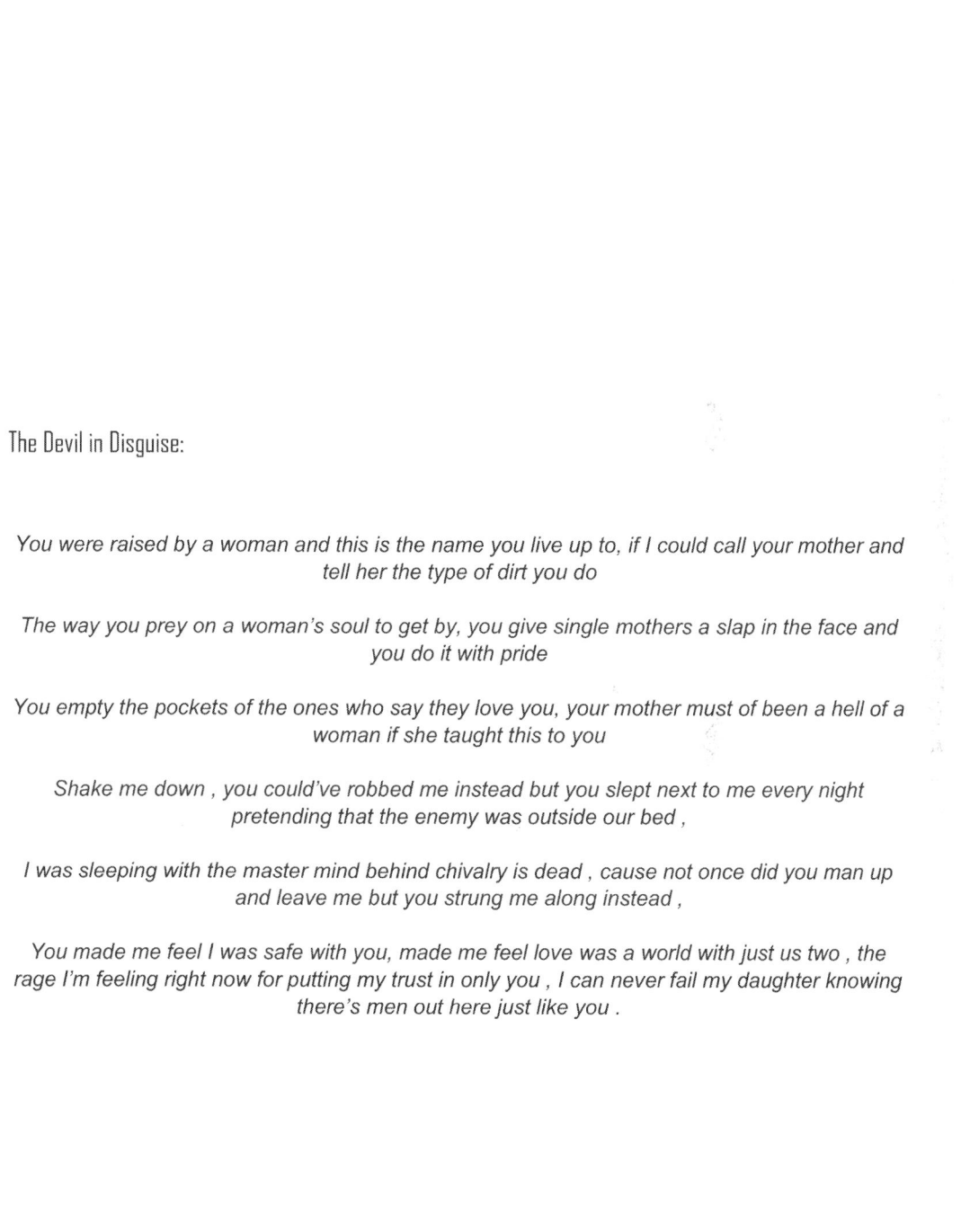

You were raised by a woman and this is the name you live up to, if I could call your mother and tell her the type of dirt you do

The way you prey on a woman's soul to get by, you give single mothers a slap in the face and you do it with pride

You empty the pockets of the ones who say they love you, your mother must of been a hell of a woman if she taught this to you

Shake me down , you could've robbed me instead but you slept next to me every night pretending that the enemy was outside our bed ,

I was sleeping with the master mind behind chivalry is dead , cause not once did you man up and leave me but you strung me along instead ,

You made me feel I was safe with you, made me feel love was a world with just us two , the rage I'm feeling right now for putting my trust in only you , I can never fail my daughter knowing there's men out here just like you .

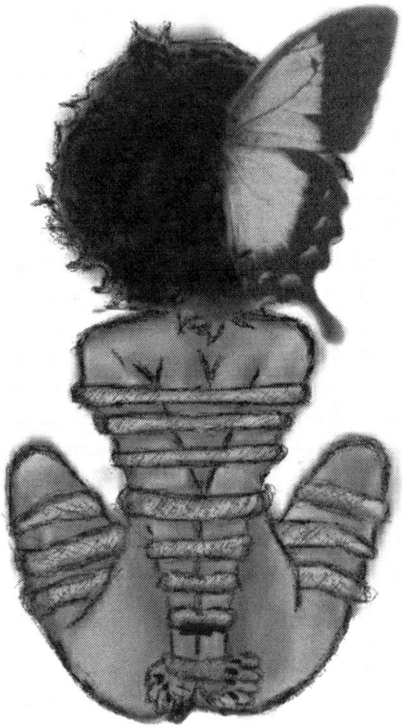

~ When we do not have the answers, we tend to believe anything that makes us feel good, trust your gut, outweigh your options. We all have options.

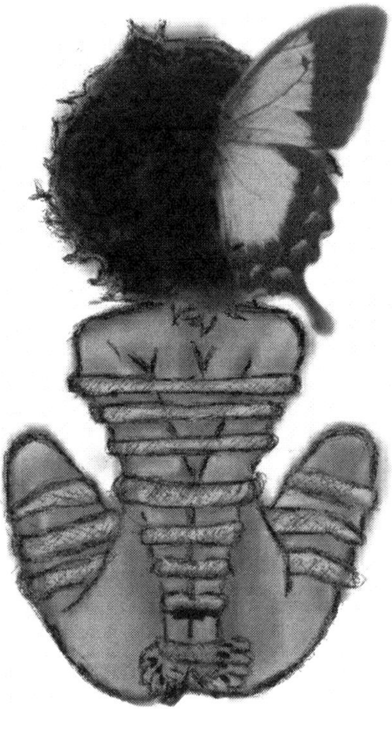

What's Love?

To all the men I loved it was never my intentions to hurt you, to love and be loved was the mission when it came to you .

I came from love so that's all I wanted to give you

but you had other plans ,

My love was deep I had it written on my thighs , my love was sweet I told no lies , I was in it for the long run and I saw a future with all of you , but my clock was ticking on your hands if we speaking truths

I wanted to give something you were never given ,
I wanted to live a different way you were living , I seen above and beyond the moon and stars ,

I never expected us to crash cause Real love , was what was given on my part

My love was unconditional I would fix every part of me , my love was never reciprocated but I kept chasing

Loyalty was what I promised you , so I broke my back to see it through , I was so ready for love that I settled for you ,

I had to experience to understand . that if a man really loves you, he will be a man, I was not the wife I thought you chose... I overextended my soul by being a wife... playing a girlfriend roll.

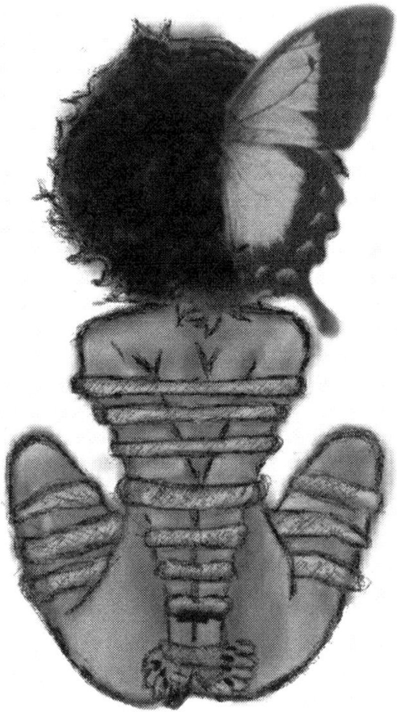

20:12

Here's a letter to my lover , you were like a lifetime brother, I'm sorry I lead you on, I misguided you ,

You didn't call me , why'd you stop calling ; that was the toughest shit you had to put me through

Excited you , lied to you ; had you all in my business , but you never loved from a distance , now it's fuck you and your feelings well,

The Sad thing is you're still hurt about it , this love wasn't meant to be

You became a piece in my diary, those feelings don't sit right with me , I'm constantly losing sleep, behind your memory ,

a one sided love, now incomplete

Move on . Release me.

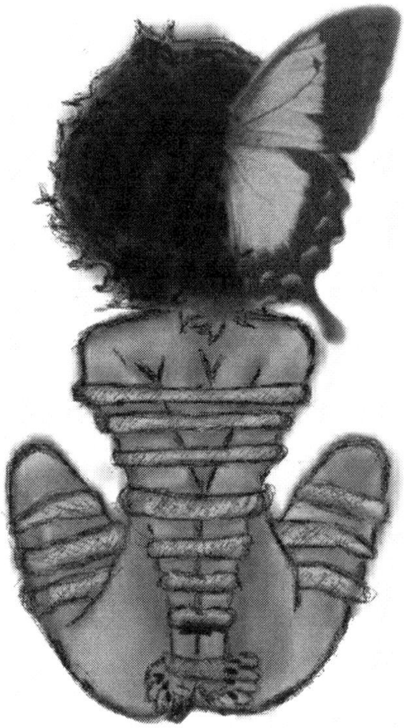

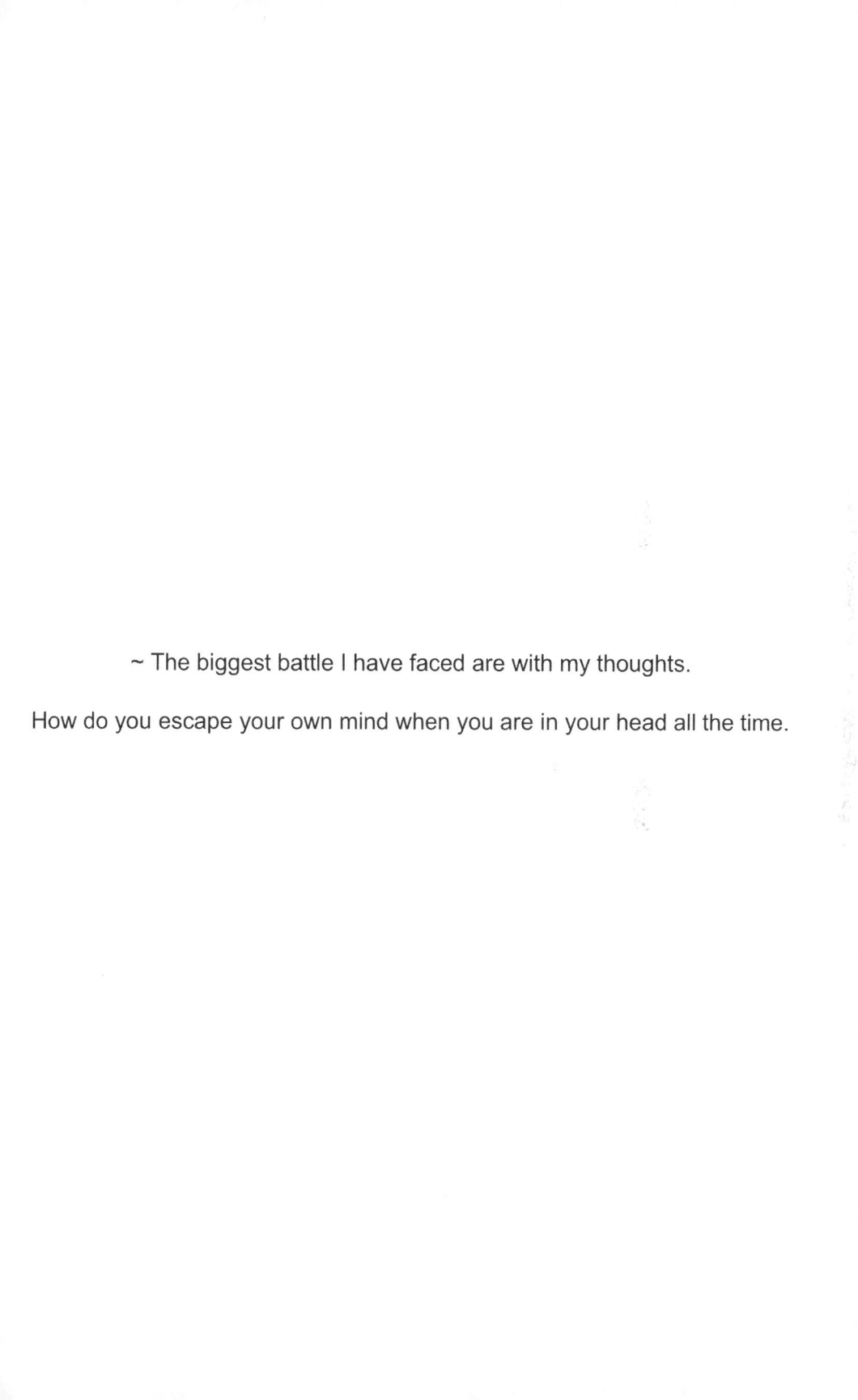

~ The biggest battle I have faced are with my thoughts.

How do you escape your own mind when you are in your head all the time.

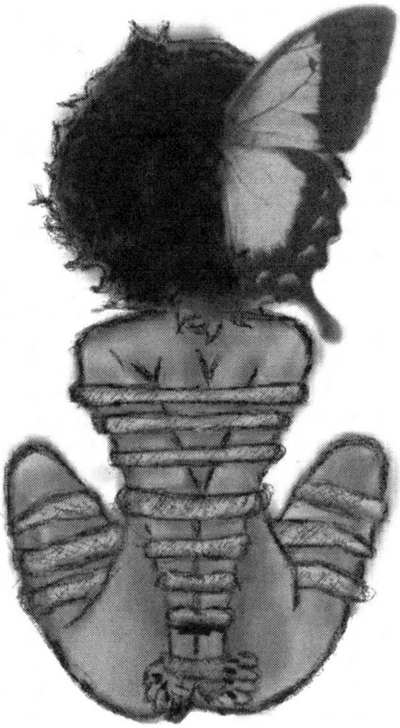

Existing:

*Dear self-come home there's still room for you here
I removed the hurt, the pain the baggage is cleared
I washed away the people you wanted to forget , I cleaned up the mess it no longer exist , I cleaned out the closet I'm for sure this time*

*Dear self-come home I promise it's you and I ;
Don't mistake our world to be what it was before , we healed each other, it no longer hurts our core*

Dear self-come home try speaking to me , you can't get lost in depression you may never come back you see , you can't battle that anxiety if we don't meet somewhere in between

*Dear self I understand you ,
Dear self-it's Me.*

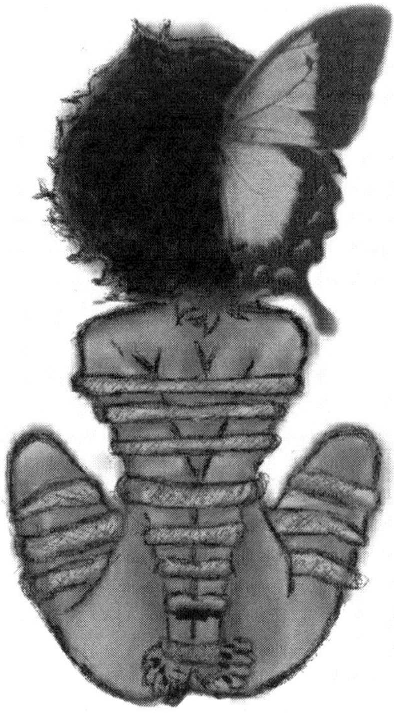

~ I move too efficiently to wait for people to catch up.

I am not waiting for anybody.

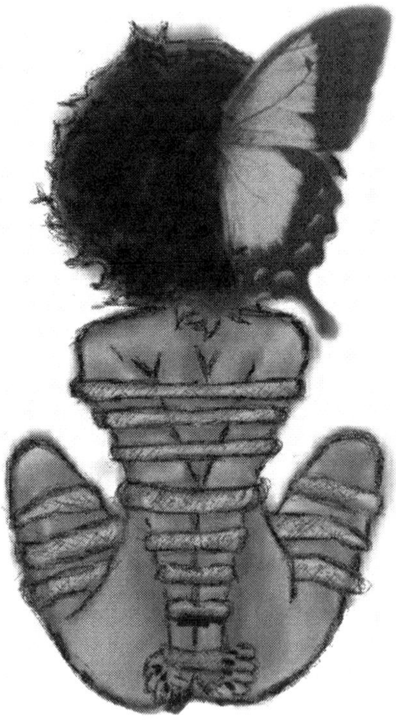

~ What is the point of being loyal in a generation that is built off lies.

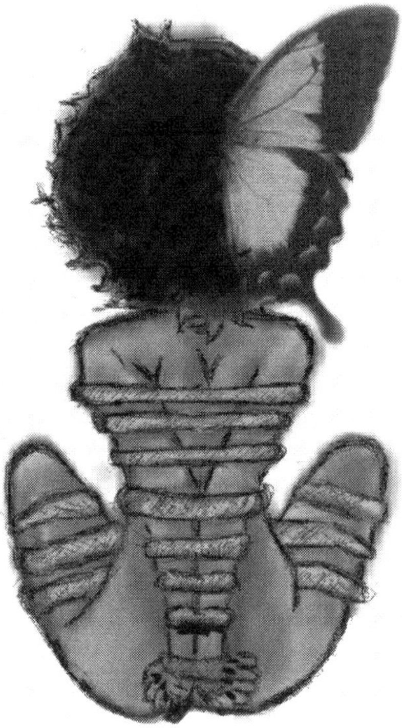

Never Be:

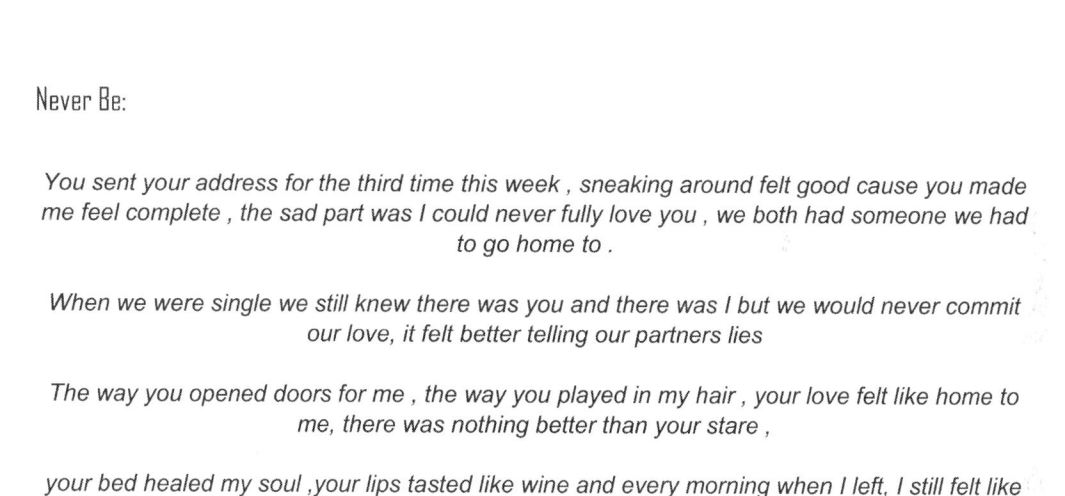

You sent your address for the third time this week , sneaking around felt good cause you made me feel complete , the sad part was I could never fully love you , we both had someone we had to go home to .

When we were single we still knew there was you and there was I but we would never commit our love, it felt better telling our partners lies

The way you opened doors for me , the way you played in my hair , your love felt like home to me, there was nothing better than your stare ,

your bed healed my soul ,your lips tasted like wine and every morning when I left, I still felt like you were just mine

I knew I loved you a little more than I should when I started comparing reasons why I couldn't be the one .

I knew you loved me a little more than you should when you said you'll wait till I was done having my fun ;

but we knew . We could never be each other's only one.

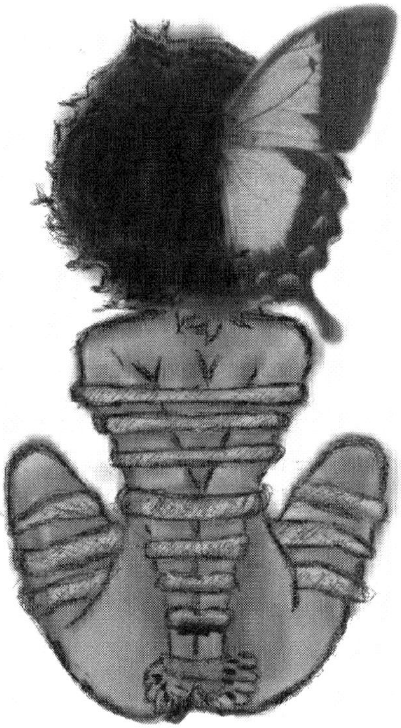

Lie to Me:

We spoke of our problems to one another and promised to never be what our past or last made us hate, I confided in you enough to lay it all on the line and promised to be the last woman you would "date" I saw a future beyond what you gave to me but look at what you stole , I thought my heart was healed but you left me wounded and left me no choice to feel less than anything whole

I won't ask why me cause that will give you too much power , I won't think about the good times cause that love story wasn't ours , I like to think destiny is what you make it but sometimes interactions are already written ,

I couldn't see that you weren't meant for me and I wasn't meant for you but there was a bigger picture

I asked myself a thousand times where did I go wrong, I blamed myself with a thousand lies of why my life couldn't go on

I told myself if I made you hurt the same way I felt from beginning to end that maybe just maybe you'll feel the emptiness I felt and we would be back together again

But why chase something that never wanted to be kept , why long for a heart that had no room for you when yours already been shelved

Late night thoughts of you .

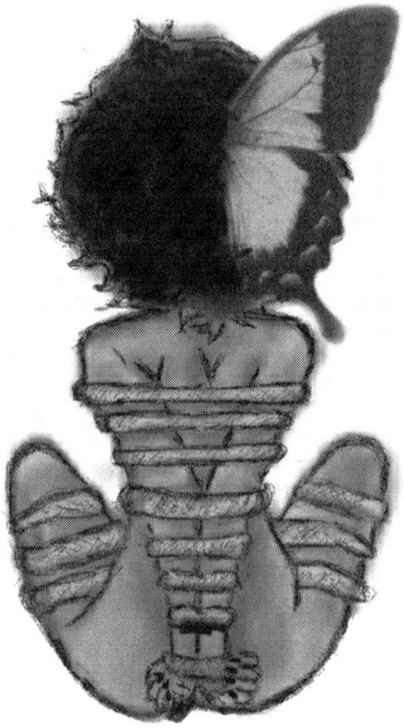

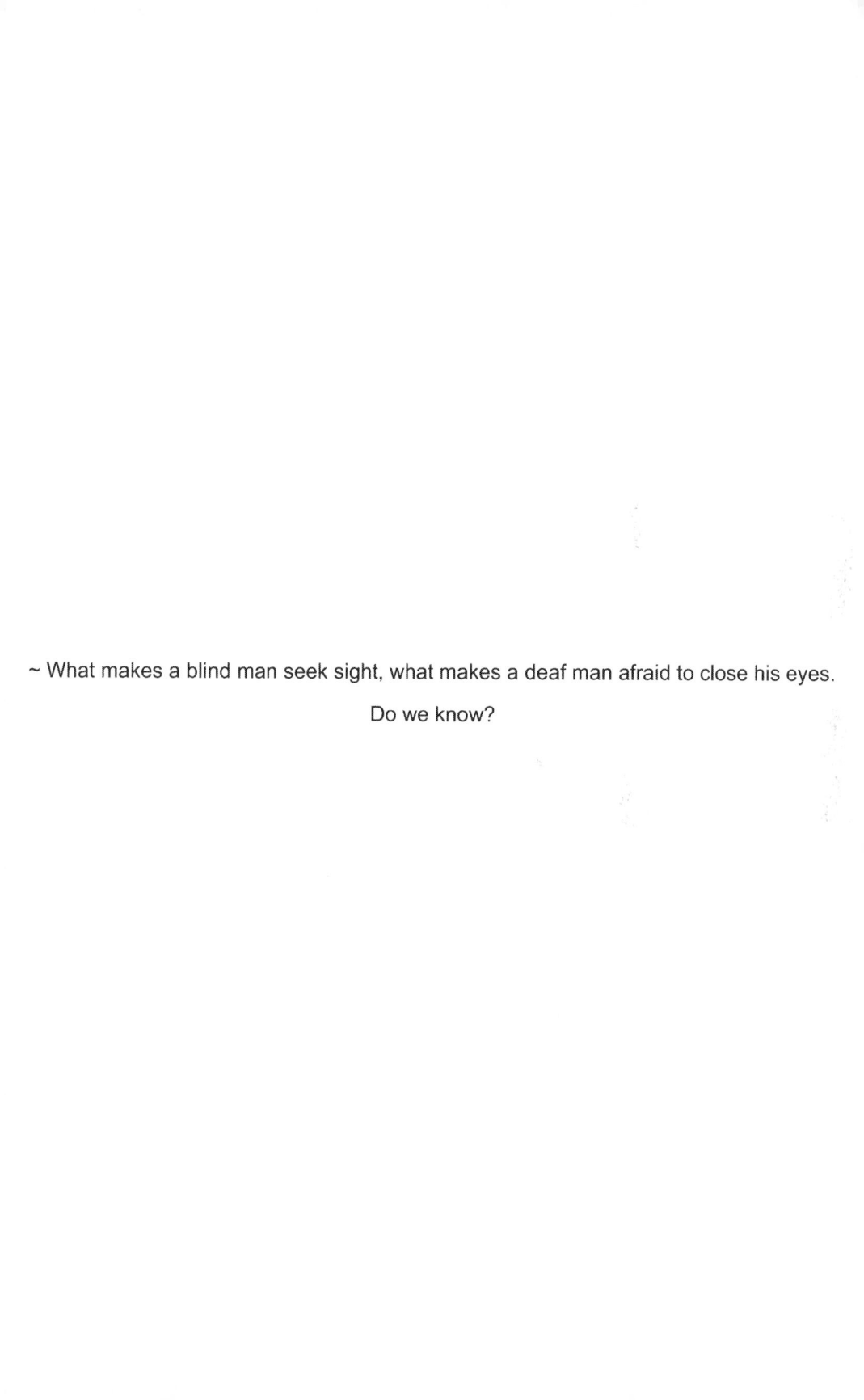

~ What makes a blind man seek sight, what makes a deaf man afraid to close his eyes.

Do we know?

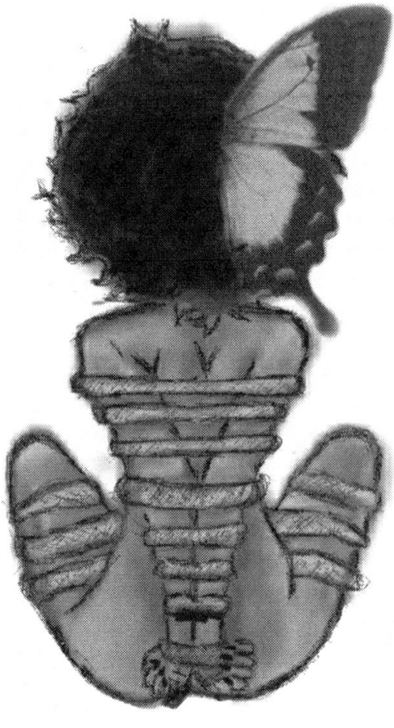

Third Person:

I saw myself as you
and I admit it's weird to say,
I smelled Your cologne..
your hands were my hands your face was my face , I got to experience what it felt like to be you for a day , I inhaled your problems and I felt your pain

I see you with a different set of eyes after all that intake , I felt the weight of the world on your shoulders and the things you don't say ...

I felt the tears on your skin the ones you hide and pretend
Men don't cry —but they do
And everything you did to women I seen the hurt in you ,

I can never look at you the same cause I walked enough miles in your shoes to say , I was disgusted , lustful and turned up my role play ,
I got to understand the role of a man for a day , but you could never know what it feels like to be she , the victim mindset y'all walk around with but with nothing to plead , the heartbreak you cause , the disparity you leave ...
I have nothing to spare , I seen with my own eyes you have no sympathy ,

it's a dog eat dog world where men still believe Eve was the true enemy,

y'all make loving a woman feel so damn cruel but want to be spoken highly of in a room where women are seen second to you
I opened up my third eye in third person , you can't heal a man you got to let that man heal himself to understand the woman
is truly a blessing .

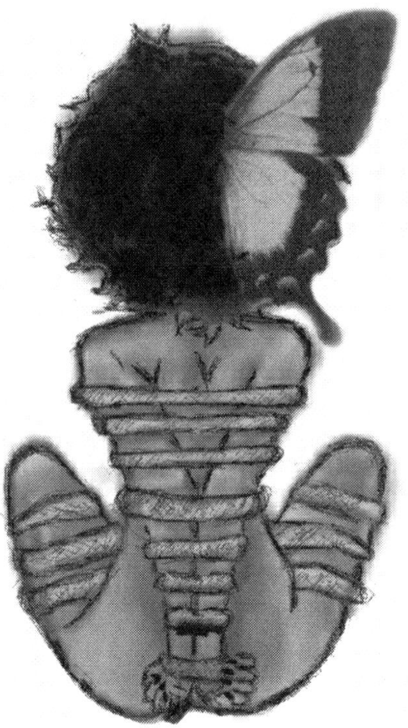

Look at what you Stole:

You stole my innocence when I saw the light in you , you raised your hand to me and showed me the demon in you, I held on for years thinking I can change your ways , I wasn't your mother but I made raising you my position to play ,

I made excuses for you cause nobody could see what I seen, I labeled you sick when the truth was you loved controlling someone as weak as me

I babied your efforts and always gave myself the short end of the stick, I became paranoid on top of depression, uninterested , now I'm erasing messages.. this shit made me sick

I was afraid of you and limited myself to be exactly what you needed , I became your puppet and every day I wanted out but I told myself your love was what I needed

Look at what you stole from me do you see the things you've done, I'm not the same anymore my worst fears I lived in but not once did I run

Look at what you stole from me , all this time I could've been ahead although your abuse didn't kill me the woman I once knew was better off dead ..

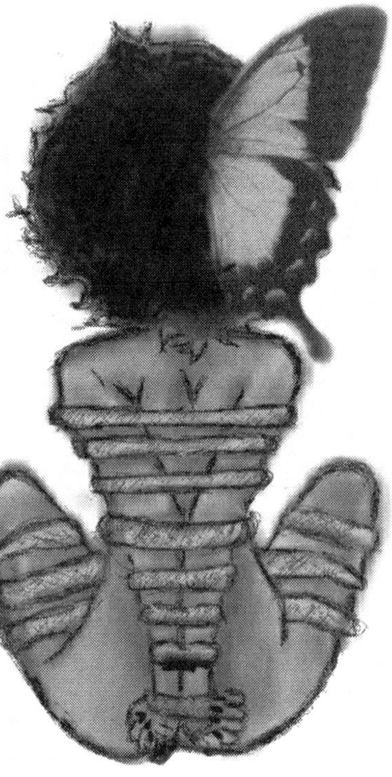

~ Not once did I stop crying, I always felt my heart was too big to be here, I gave way too much, I loved way too hard, but I never doubted that one day someone would appreciate me

One day ...

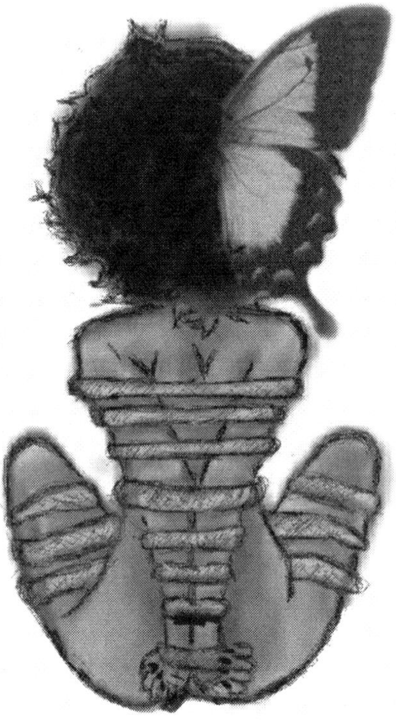

STILL HERE:

If I knew the last time I saw you would be the last time, I would of hugged you tighter, I would've kissed you longer, I would've looked back instead of feeling like everything was okay, I know that's some crazy shit to say but who would've knew I would lose my friend, that became my man, just for that love to fade away and never hear from him again..

I hope you find the peace I couldn't give you, the love you felt you didn't receive, a heart that feels warm, and lips better than mine that gives you the climax you need

I started to write out my feelings and started to think of you, tonight it was something I needed and the void was you , and even when I feel like I'm healing there you appear .. I remember your smile, your laugh, your touch and wanted to pull you near, and with all the hate in the world, it brought tears to my face cause how can you mourn someone who is not dead in the first place.

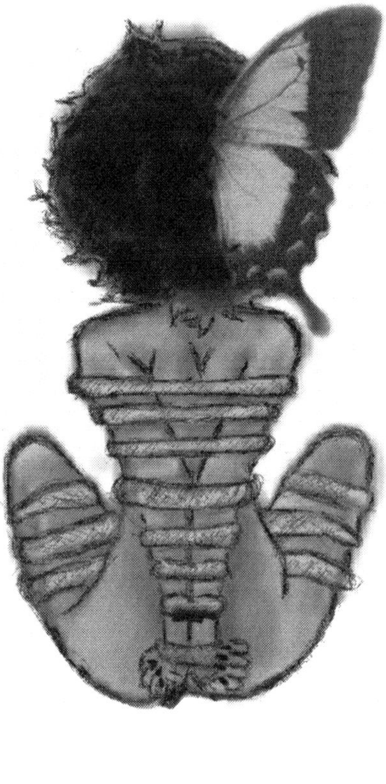

Heartbroken:

I was never afraid to get my heart broken , I was only afraid of not being prepared , because what if I fell in love so deep and I didn't see the end coming near

What if that man stopped loving me before I was ready to stop loving him , What if that man no longer poured into me while I continued to pour into him

What if I saw the fairy tale ending with wedding bells and crooked smiles While he imagined his life with another woman and his love started to fade after while

I was never afraid of getting my heart broken , I was only afraid of not being prepared because why would the man I loved so much heart no longer want me near.

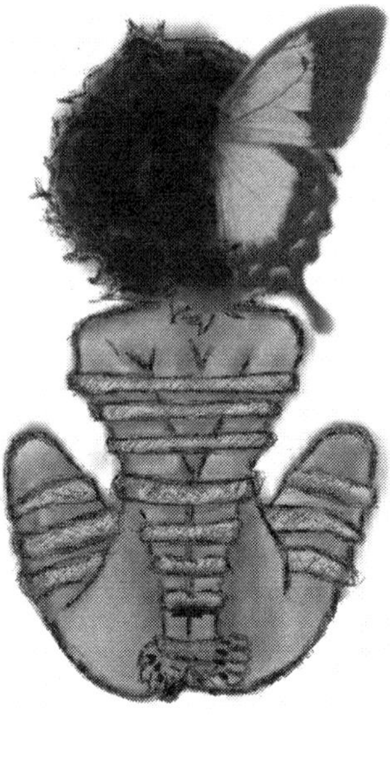

I begged for you...
to a point i cried and couldn't feel my face , my knees were so numb from crouching in that same state ,

I questioned what was it that I done that made you feel incomplete , was I the one who made you separate yourself from me

This love shit can really give you the blues , and hit you with unexpected hurt and betrayal too from calls and text messages , to emails and Pinger messages but it never stops there the shit keeps progressing ...

I'm creeping in the dark trying to find somewhere to park I got a new car he won't notice me at all , I wonder does he give her more than he gave me .. is she meeting his mom are they sharing a damn dog

Man..

I can't stop reminiscing it's a vivid picture the color seeps out on the kitchen walls...

reminds me of the days you didn't call , reminds me of the nights I still showed up for you , reminds me of the reasons they told me let go of you but I still held on true ,
and you couldn't fight for us ?
I put ME on the line for love and I still want better for you

That night your grandmother died I was up all night too that's when I knew soul ties were deeper than just me and you ..I was looking at her picture weeping for you , I felt the emptiness in my chest like it was my family member that left a world where a man can treat a woman like this but cry for a woman like that, I'm beyond confused

I wonder can you even look at me now, do you even smile the same now, that shit still Breaks me down ... I counted too many I love yous but chose to ignore the signs, I could have saved myself of this wasted time, and if I could go back and do it all again I would just to be able to say I Love you again.

Save my Love, you will not forget my touch ...

Impacted by Love

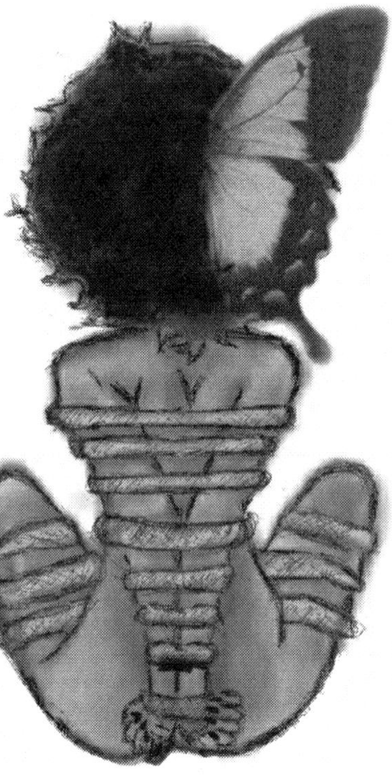

~ When I care too much I give too much, I express too much, and it never ends well ... I learned solitude is the best form of expression, you blossom more, you smile more, you hurt less ...

Practice learning to live in your Solitude, I promise you will love the YOU that you will become.

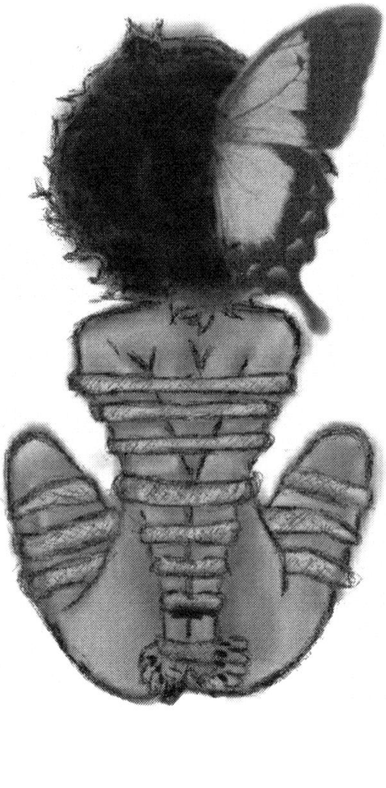

~ An unforgiving heart will always be a tainted heart.

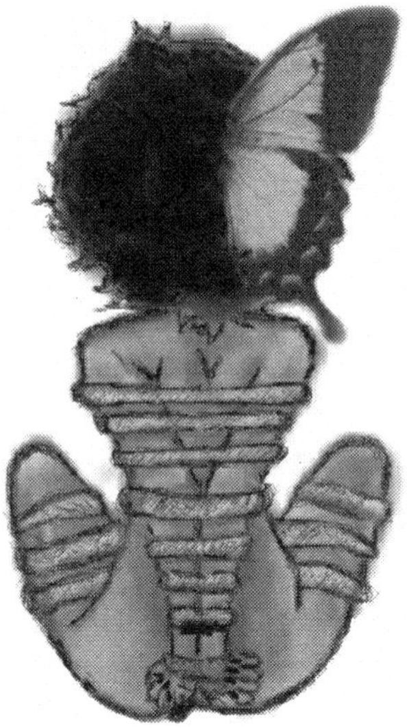

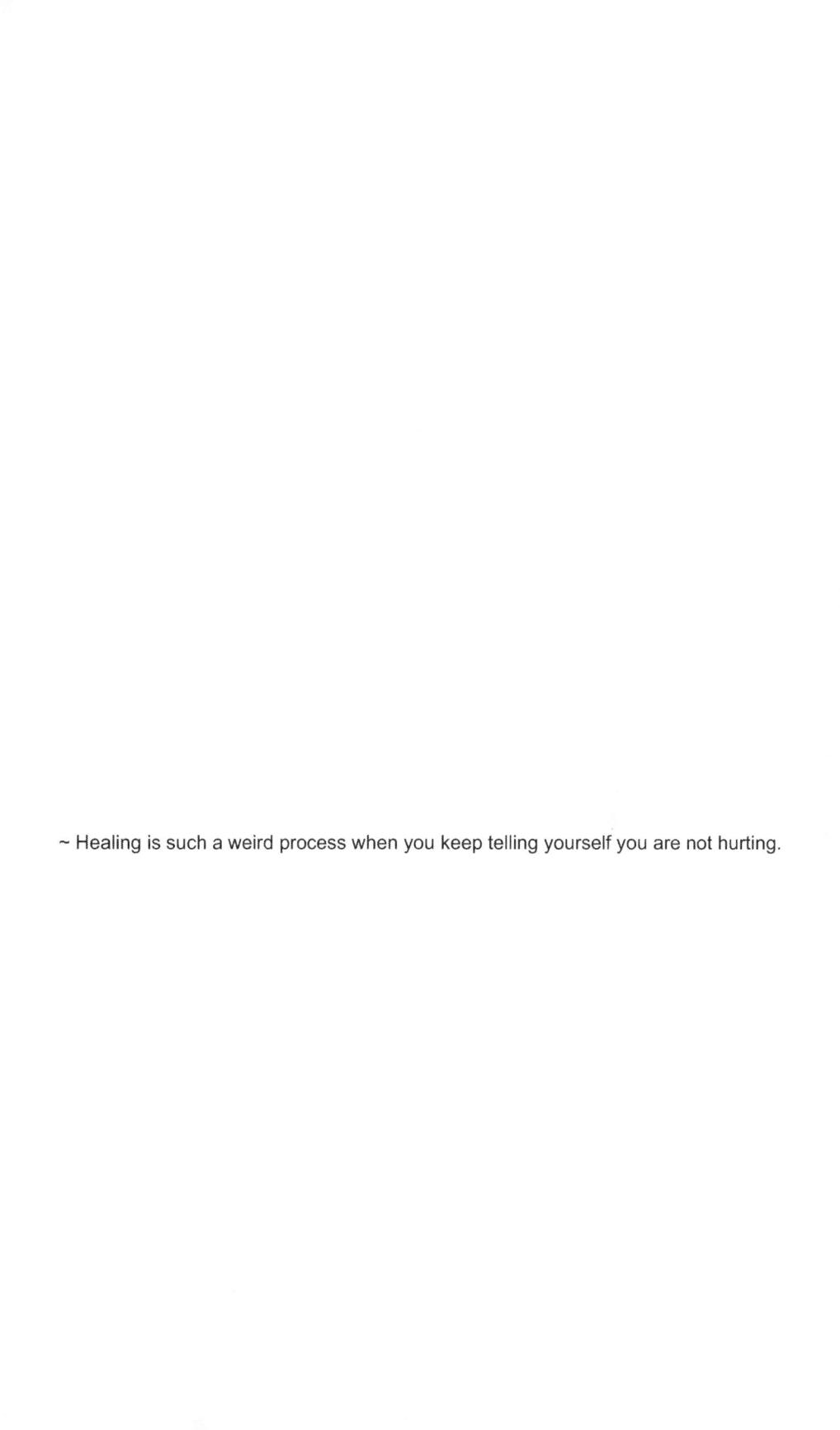

~ Healing is such a weird process when you keep telling yourself you are not hurting.

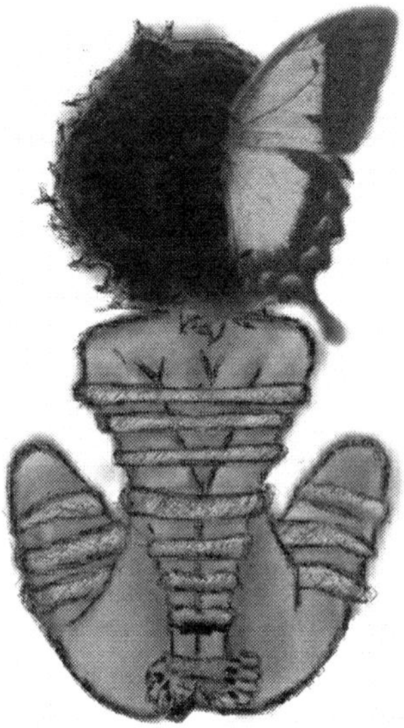

Notes:

Sometimes closure is the very thing we search for to help us sleep at night, to help our mind stop racing, to convince ourselves that maybe just maybe we can be overthinking a situation, overlooking actions that never took place to begin with.

Sometimes it is beyond words, sometimes it is beyond feelings, it becomes deeper than that.

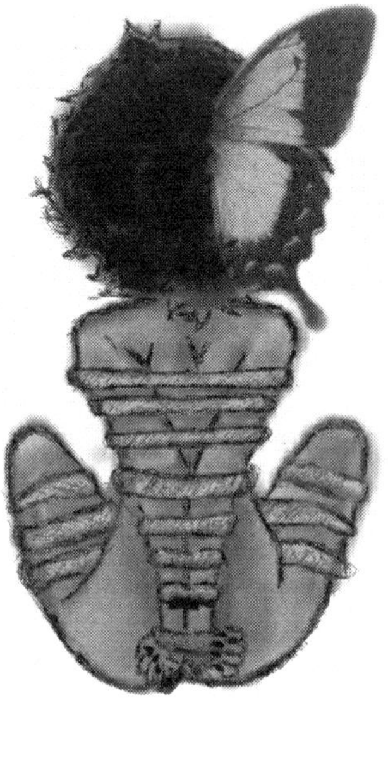

One's Imagination:

I was patient with love, I daydreamed about what a perfect love would be, what it would feel like, what it would taste like, an image only I could see.

Nobody warned me that it takes two, I thought if I imagined it, I could live it and everything I imagined would deem fit, but that wasn't true

I searched for an image, a touch, a voice only I can see. I experienced the opposite of everything I wanted and attracted unlike souls that held on to me .

I stumbled upon bare feet that had been damaged for far too long , I became the fixer cause what I imagined when it came to love was a true love song .

Nobody told me that love wasn't supposed to hurt , nobody told me that sometimes you got to leave those situations and put you first

I held on for the feelings that faded from the beginning , I begged for consistency cause I missed what it felt like but in reality I was sinking

Nobody told me let love find you, so I continued searching for "the one" and forcing others to understand the meaning...

But I learned with true love there's no limits and you'll feel complete , you won't feel exhausted cause your partner will truly know love doesn't cut deep.

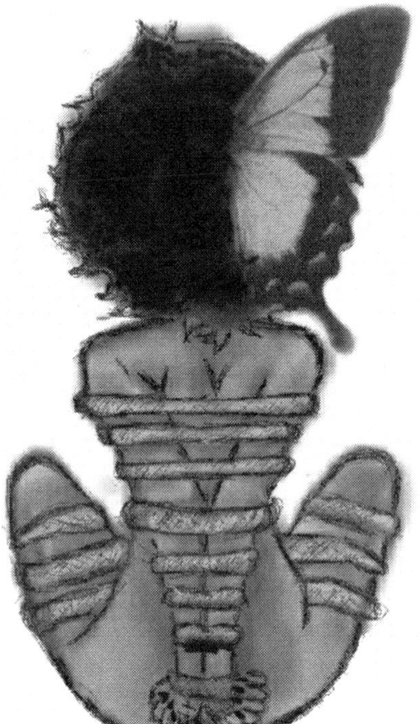

~ I Love being alone, but I hate being lonely.

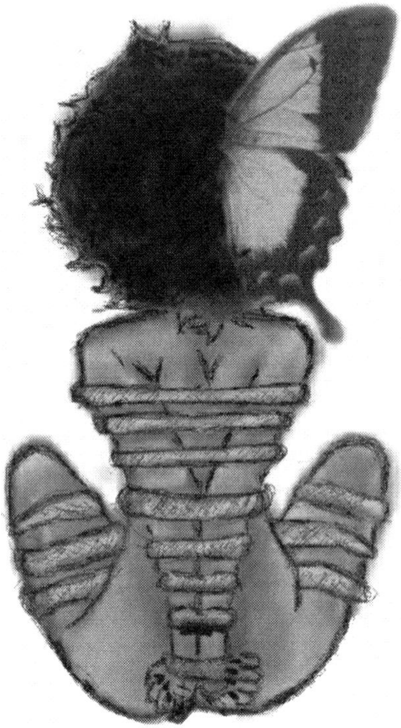

A Short Story Inside of the book,

I know what it feels like to feel like you are losing control, I know what it feels like to feel like the world would be better off without you, I know what it feels like to talk yourself down off that ledge I know what it feels like to say you will be better off dead.

But listen, if nobody understands you please understand that I do. I understand the anxiety the depression, even the moments where failed attempts felt too good to be true .

In this life we don't know what the future holds , but know that everything we experience is meant to help us grow .

If it helps any , think of it this way , ask yourself how , why and when will you show up for yourself today.

Stop letting the thoughts of others control you, stop trying to write the narrative that's been already written for you .

You don't want to be seen as weak but it's okay to cry, it's okay to take some time away from the world to keep YOU in mind , it's okay that your today didn't go as planned, it's okay that job didn't call you back again, it's okay that your parents don't understand you, it's okay that woman or man didn't chose you , it's okay you're on your 3rd glass of wine , it's okay you need a shot of whisky to pass time . It's okay you missed out on that home , it's okay you have to do things alone , I promise you it's okay to cry, I rather you let it all out now cause your future is aligned .

I don't know who needs to hear this but I'm sure I wrote this for you , this page was made special , this very page You turned to .

I can see behind that fake smile , I can see beyond the lies , did I mention I was once in your shoes ? so when I say I know what it feels like it's because I once was there too.

I felt sorry for myself because I loved too deep, I felt sorry for myself cause I repeated the same things , I felt sorry for myself when my life would spin out of control , I never appreciated myself when I was doing fine , I always channeled my fuck ups or the wrongs at the time , I never understood how things connected until one day one situation made me really understand it ,

I started to turn my negatives into positives , I stopped the woe is me and started to adapt to it , to manage it , to control it to grasp it cause yes indeed it was mine , you have full control over your body , soul , and mind .. you feed your thoughts and energy with things you want to make yourself grow, you figure out where you want to heal, why you want to heal, and you process it slow. I am no saint, but I chose to play the victim to, understand me when I say I was once in your shoes ...

Take back your life, Tap into you.

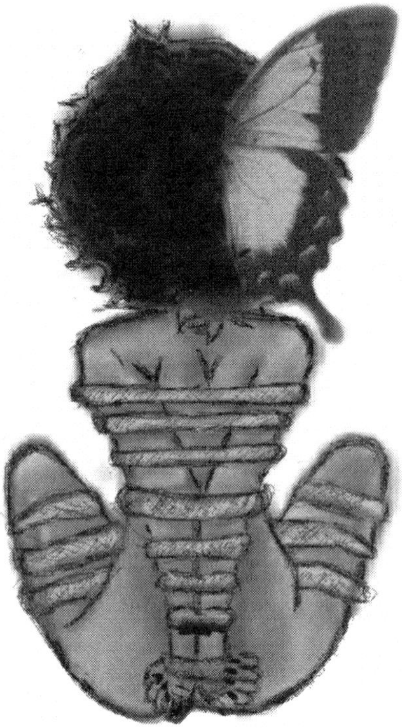

~ It is no mistake you are here today, find your purpose.

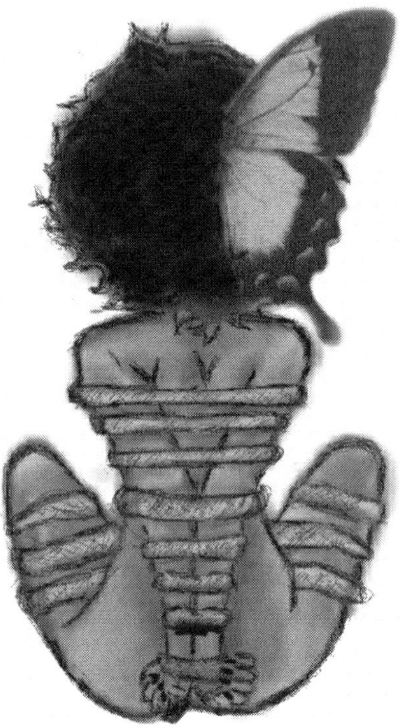

~ If we did not have experiences, we would not know exactly what we are learning from.

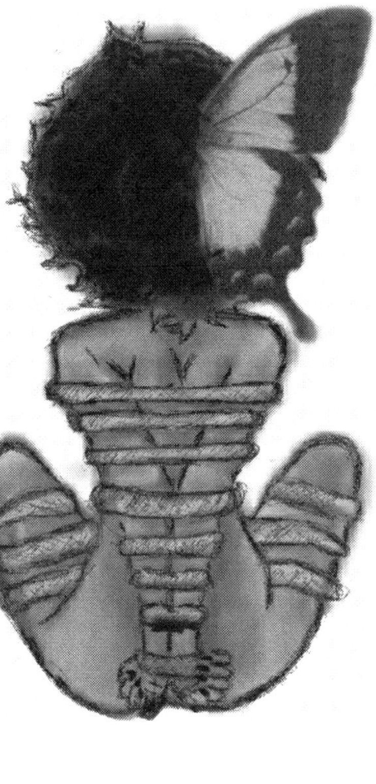

My sanity is more important than temporary feelings

I am a genuine soul; my love is so pure ...

I am an empath that takes in other people's hurt and make it my own. Sometimes I need space not for my own problems but the problems of others I chose to take in, now I am healing me from hurt that was never even mine to begin with.

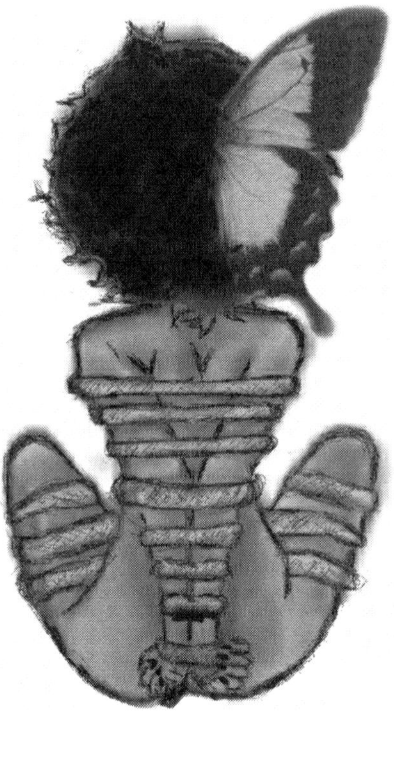

~ Somedays I wanted to love again, feel again, be me again Somedays I got that with you.

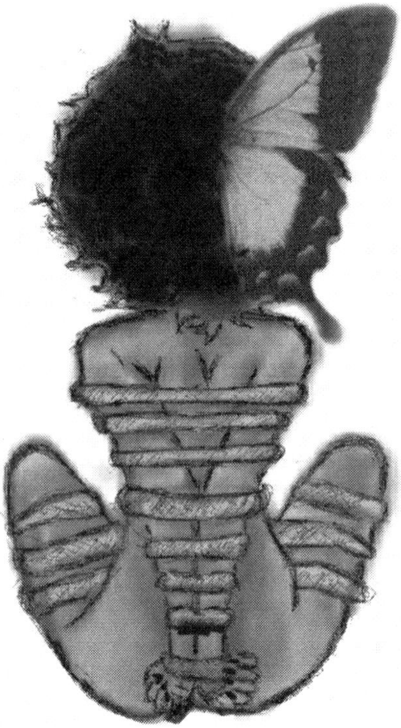

Secrets:

Your kisses against my skin made me feel brand new , your whispers in my ear , reminded me why I felt safe with you .

*Somehow you get me, that's what I always loved about you .
See Somehow you get me that's what I always loved about you .*

But let's be honest your physical appearance played a huge role , that's what Attracted me to you if you didn't know
Then you started to say all the right things , so I pushed you away , feeling like this couldn't be

Then I came back to you in due time , your scent smelled even better than the last time , your touch caressed my body in every way , your sex was amazing enough to make me stay

There was a climax when it came to you, we had no title but the title was YOU.

You showed me what it was like to be catered to, you showed me what it was like to matter to you, and even if I say I've never been in love , I can say you made me feel close enough ....

But damn he'll never know .

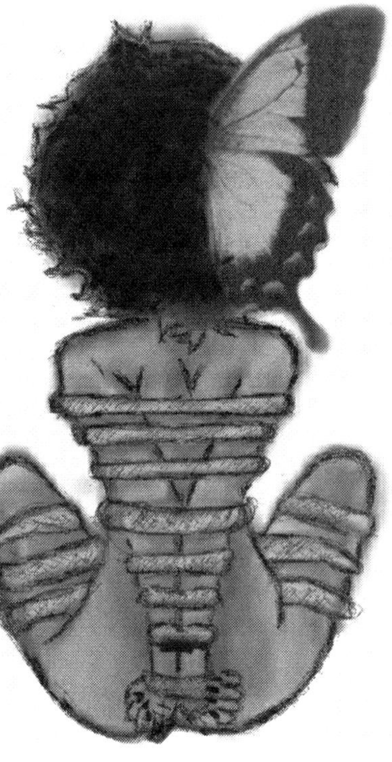

Rap Sheet:

If you got the answers I swear I'm ready to listen now ..

when you leave I feel needy , all my pride you can take it , how ?

hold me up on my feet cause this miscommunication ..must've been mistaken , and if there's a bruise for the times I felt used,

I'm covered in bruises and still covered in doubt .

Listen while I'm hungry for the right words to respond to you , I'm rambling with purpose but I'll stop talking soon .

I've been scared of the possibilities many reasons there's no truths , I followed the roads and they all led back to you , so I have to heal my soul cause I'm stuck and can't move on , so talk to me now cause I'll stop talking and run,

you'll search for me when I'm gone so I'm giving you the option now , I'm ready to listen our problems came in twos , diffused and watered down but I'll give you space to satisfy your views.

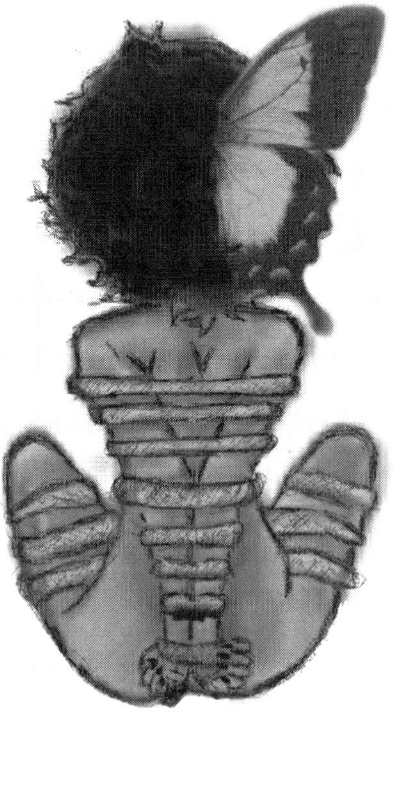

~ Sometimes we create this false reality, we live in an illusion which leaves us searching for the idea of what something could be or could have been, let's stop doing that because it is hurting us more than we think.

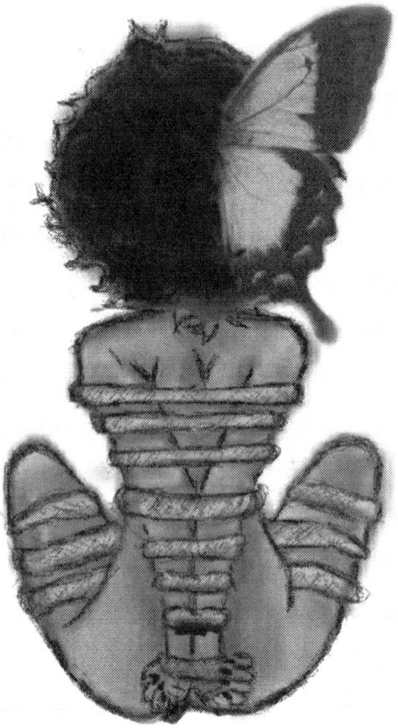

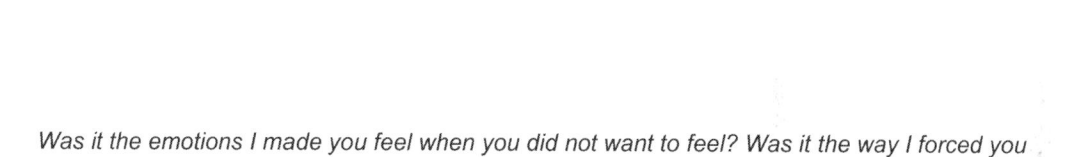

Sink:

Was it the emotions I made you feel when you did not want to feel? Was it the way I forced you to express things you wanted to keep to yourself , I cared and it hurts to lie.

Although we grew apart there was something that still made me hold on to you , was it the what if's , the could haves and the should haves that made me feel you had a place in my life

It's okay if you hate me , cause I'll forever love you.
It's okay if you regret me, cause someone has to.

I learned from you and you showed me it wasn't real . I felt for you, now I am forced to heal, I cried with you and that shit felt deep. and every moment I spent with you has me questioning everything ...

If you hate me at least tell me why, why did you choose me to break from the inside, why did I have to be the test, why pick me? I need you to confess, no words can express the emptiness I feel, if I could just get all my time back maybe these wounds will seal

I am drowning in you.

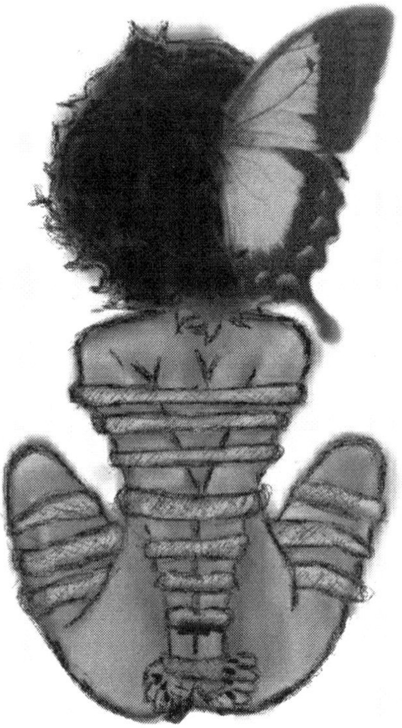

Descriptions:

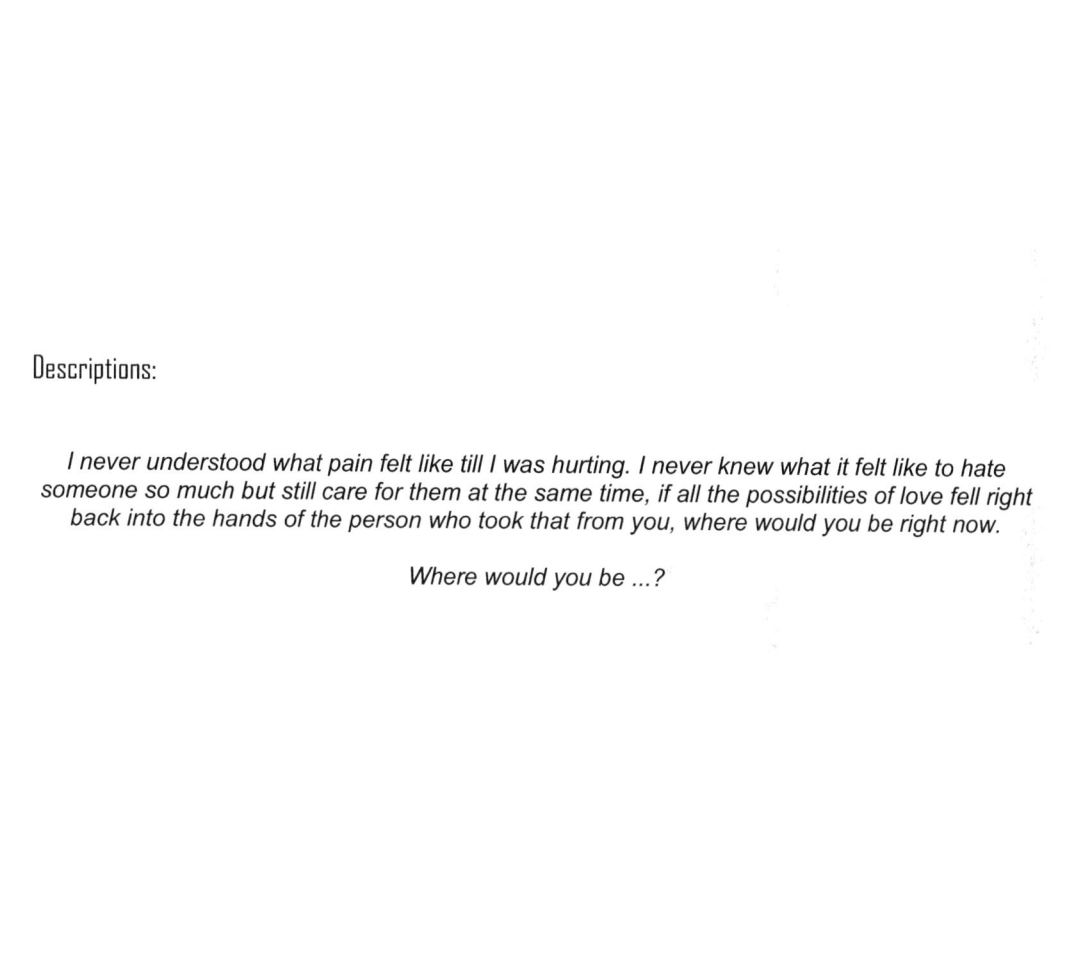

I never understood what pain felt like till I was hurting. I never knew what it felt like to hate someone so much but still care for them at the same time, if all the possibilities of love fell right back into the hands of the person who took that from you, where would you be right now.

Where would you be ...?

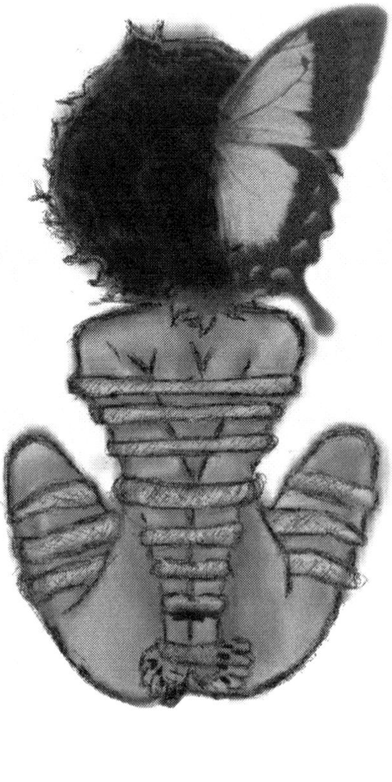

Empty:

*Give me — me back I want to smile again ,
I want to know what it feels like to fall in love with another man ,
I want to have hope that the next person won't do me wrong ,
I want to trust again cause the overthinking has become too strong*

Give me —me back you made me feel insecure, it's not like I don't feel pretty enough but the repeated questions is what occurs

*Give me — me back I want to feel whole, I poured out my eyes to you, gave up my life for you ,
lied for you
and you STILL
Found it in yourself to leave me ... look at what you stole ,
and sometimes I feel too needy , your damage left me empty , heart barely breathing ,
you could've left me alone .*

But I made a promise to myself that no man (never again) will take away what you stole

I'm taking time to make ME whole.

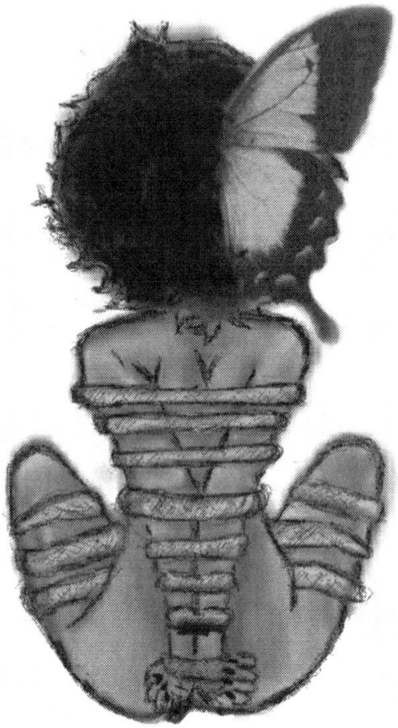

My Last Goodbye:

Why continue to hold on to someone if it's not what you want , you sent me 2 text messages in one day and barely answered your phone , when I questioned you, you replied you were tired and sleep , you always would tell me "Babe , it's been a long week" .

When I asked for your time you made me feel like I was begging,
I felt like I was bothering you and I couldn't stand it ,
but why not walk away instead of stringing me along , why make my love deeper for you if you were just going to move on ..

I've re-read our text messages from beginning to end , I still ask myself how didn't I see this failed love descend

I'm still making excuses for you in my mind , I'm looking at this shit like it was written in black and white.
You got over on the little lies I give you that , but I still somehow managed to take you right back

This is my Last Goodbye but I have a question for you
"When your daughter grows up would you want her to choose
(a you)"

Would you want her to be damaged by the lies of a man,

would you want her crying to you cause she doesn't understand ,

would you want her waiting on a reply back ,

would you want her asking "daddy why did he do me like that"

would you want her going through what you put me through,

would you want the emptiness for her like the emptiness I had for you ...

I ask that you hold on to your daughter,
cause karma comes in twos,
and you'll be a fool to believe,
it's done with you .

Goodbye Forever .

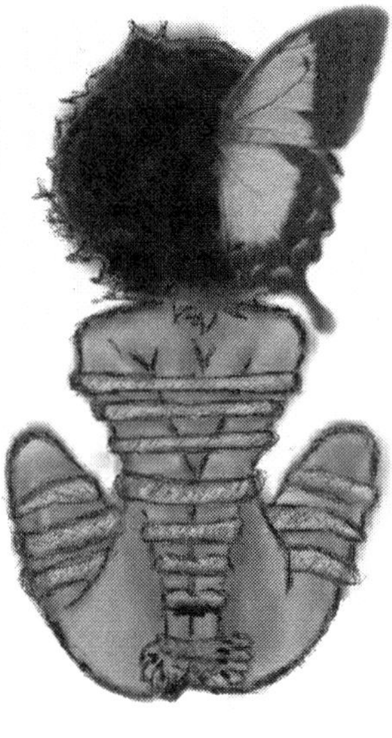

*Letting go of the things that once made us happy will never be easy.
Sometimes you'll have to relive memories you don't want to relive , face feelings you don't want to feel , and get rid of baggage and damage you don't want to carry.*

It gets easier by the day, cause the more you forgive you'll forget and you will no longer ask "why me "

Start Taking that walk toward a Fresh Start and a healed heart .

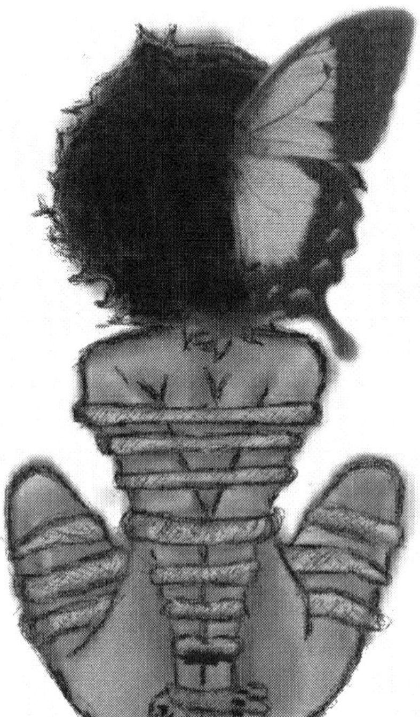

First Step:

I thought I would be angry today when I came across pictures of you, I thought tears would fall from my eyes but I'm healed from you , I want happiness for you, love for you and more than anything peace for you .

I was always afraid to say that out loud , I thought it would make me look weak, actually there's a few things I didn't speak on but I guess it's my time to speak

When I pass by the restaurants where we once shared our love I feel good,

when I hear your name I'm no longer holding a grudge ,

when I smell your cologne my body no longer screams

If this is what peace feels like , then Lord you did your thing ...

I'm proud I gave my love the way that I did , I don't hold back with any regrets .. it takes a strong woman to admit it the way that I did

This is the first step to healing. Laying it all out on the table for myself to see, I am no longer lying to myself to protect my own feelings ... and that is when I knew finding my joy again would be a good thing.

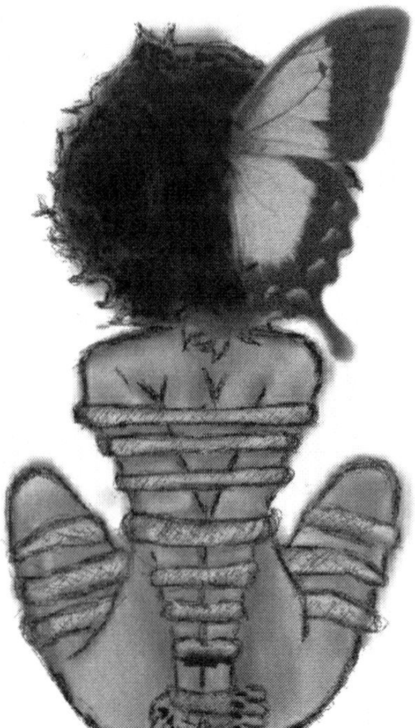

~ Sometimes we must meet ourselves halfway to get to that place of comfort we been longing for, it is the fight with your mind and body but once they meet, growth becomes a beautiful place.

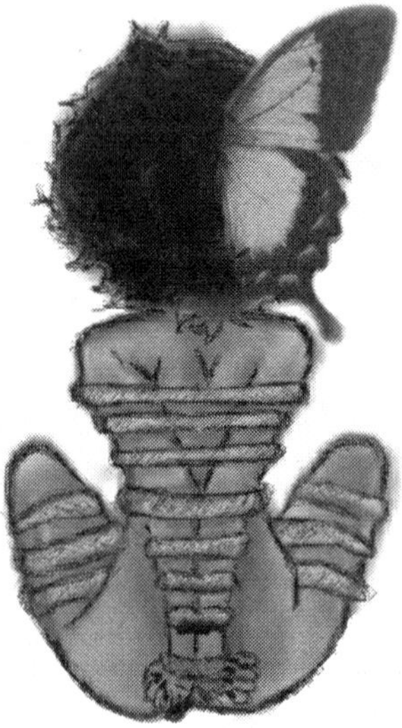

I give love because I come from love ...

I promise to never stop doing that or being that for someone else just because someone did not know how to love me right.

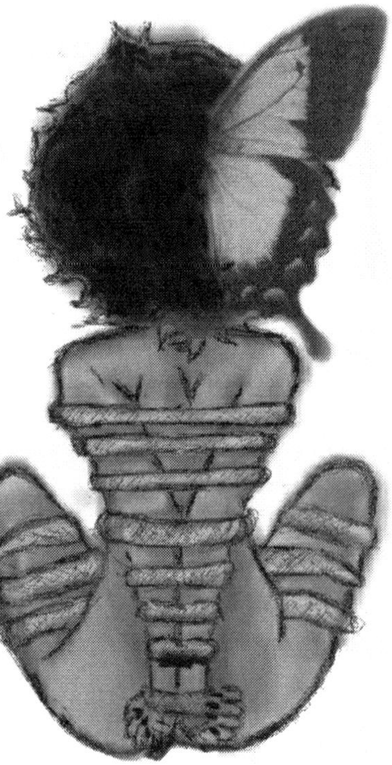

Loose Ends:

A Statement to fight your fight and stand in your truth.

So here I wrote out my lines for you, I revealed what made me weak, weep and the things I thought destroyed me..
I confronted love , heartbreak and hurt right in the face , I wrote out my feelings to comfort those who have ever felt the same .

I hope you found your page or pages that you related to, I hope your heart is full or your questions were answered when reading every page ...

Always remember that love is in the heart of the beholder don't EVER give up on someone without trying but don't ever stay out of guilt, weakness, or the need to feel

We've all been damaged , we've all over stayed our welcome when it came to love, continue to give love and in due time you'll receive it from the right one .

Thanks for supporting me ,
I give my love .

-L.D.Lovejoy

B . A . R . E .

Being Alone Reveals Emotion

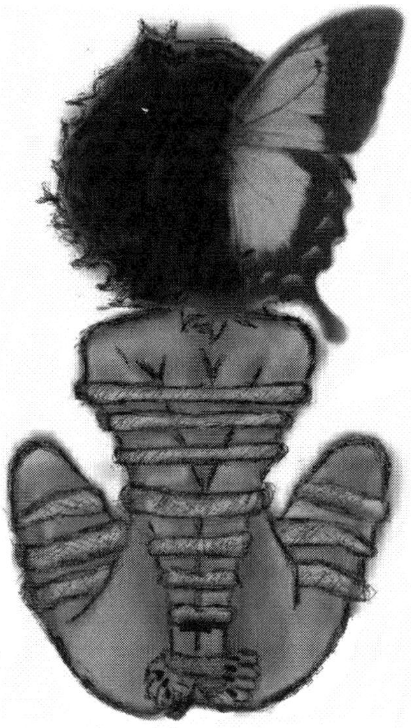

Made in the USA
Columbia, SC
03 August 2025

ee79a388-63a2-4ab3-8c72-ff75e66a383cR01